# NOTES ON THE RETURN TO THE ISLAND

Also by Bonafide Rojas

*Renovatio*
*When The City Sleeps*
*Pelo Bueno*

# Notes On
# The Return
# To The Island

bonafide rojas

GRAND
CONCOURSE
PRESS

Grand Concourse Press
www.grandconcoursepress.com

Published in the United States by:
Grand Concourse Press

First Edition
ISBN-13: 978-0692860533
ISBN-10: 0692860533

*Many thanks to the editors of the following publications
in which some of these poems appeared:*

*Manetca!:* "30 Ways Of Looking At A Nuyorican,"
"Playa Sucia To El Local," & "The New Routine"

*Late Orphan Project:* "Miguel & The Ocean,"
& "Last Night In Santurce"

*TheThePoetryBlog Series:* "Inside the Museum of Natural History,"
& "30 Ways Of Looking At A Nuyorican"

*For*
*Lefty & Fela*

# CONTENTS

# NOTES ON THE RETURN TO THE ISLAND

I.

# AT THE TOP OF EL MORRO

I.
today we celebrate
the death of the past
that has haunted us
since the very beginning

we mourn the living
& wash our hands
of all the names
that tried to destroy us

the ventriloquist is on stage
we don't care about
a puppet government
politicians, governors
or presidents because
we can see the strings

the laws they pass rhyme with
eradication, annihilation & extinction

it taste like rotten apples

II.
these money grubbing bastards
are scared of being bankrupt
yet they owe billions to other countries
& say we owe billions to them
they're delusional, their heart is weak
their vision of the future is bleak
like an unnamed catastrophe
that has scourged the island to
a burnt-out cinder inhabited
by the corpses of dead corporations
our sky is shrouded by toxic dust particulates

a gold coin is placed on our tongues
we hold oil in our cheeks
we light candles for the people
who never came back from war

the puppet government
wears wood dentures
poison the water we drink
chemically create the food we eat
sharpen their silver spoons
pour wine into the skulls of dead monarchs
       & they stand there
         hideous & forsaken
         think of us as cattle
         rattle, profit, loss, consumer

we are not here for the slaughter
we are not here for the slaughter

III.
when facing down the barrel of a gun
hope they're a bad shot
hope they're not just following orders
hope you look like their child
hope they had an amazing day
hope they realize you're not the person they're looking for
hope they know this is not the old wild west
hope god intervenes even though you are an atheist
hope they love your luxurious hair
hope you're not holding a wallet
hope you're not holding a water pistol
hope you don't have candy in your hand
hope you don't get stopped at a traffic light
hope they don't have fear on their breath
hope they don't think you're a terrorist
hope they don't think you're a communist
hope they don't think you're an independentista
hope they have some humanity left in their trigger finger

hope they haven't been trained for this
hope this is not a reoccurring dream
hope you wake up from this alive

IV.
at the top of el morro[1]
you can see politicians
walking around smelling
like corruption & massacre
they hold bone marrow in their glasses
bow before their own skeletons
eat the bark off dead cherry trees
take a casual walk in a cemetery
crushing the bones of dead nationalistas
their mouths full of declarations smell like vomit
carry blood in their pockets
brush their teeth with scalpels
watch the closed circuit destruction
of palestine, chicago, baltimore & vieques[2]
they laugh at the death tolls
eat their own shit to survive
sacrifice babies for immortality
destroy the dignity of the poor
paint their self portraits with maggots
lay their bodies on dead goats
waiting to be resurrected
when the stockmarket crashes again
so they can sink their teeth into
everything, everywhere, & everyone

at the top of el morro
we wash our hands of their existence
we wash our hands of their name
& we walk into the ocean
& bathe ourselves in freedom.

# II.
# AQUÍ/ALLÁ

# WELCOME TO THE JUNGLE

the plane lands
i'm back on
the island of my
parent's birth
there's are a lot
of american flags here
lots of guns too

welcome to the jungle
is playing on my headphones
i'm trying to block out
the intense heat
vibrating off the concrete
i know where i am
this is not new
a bit rare though
it's like a dream
or more like a memory
of a five year old rojas
living in levittown[3]
& a ten year old rojas
spending summers
in bayamón[4]

growing up on this island
taught me lessons
that i didn't understand
there was fun, games
but also bad nicknames
that lasted a few years
before i stopped giving a shit

ten years later
i saw how tourism
controlled the island
transformed it from

forefront to storefront
fancy commercials with
the word enchanted everywhere
everything needs a marketing scheme
new branding, a mission & a slogan
the united states pushed their
propaganda deep into our mouths
the military brought
puerto rico to its knees

i watch them bleed
then i turn the channel
i've been so disconnected
that i thought that
this wasn't my problem
every trip i tried to
reconnect myself
i would go out west where
there were no bright lights
pero estrellas to stare at
montañas to climbs
& coquis to listen to

i watch the military
crawl on their bellies
like serpentine demigods
offering people to take bites
from the big apple

i am asked to kill my sister because
she was considered dangerous
i am asked to turn my mother in
for being an independentista
& rallying against the government

this enchanted island
captured through a war
has had experiments injected upon

my neighbors bootstrapped operated
assimilated everyone
with american fast food
it made me unaware of
the patria of my tongue
the bomba y plena[5]
of my fists & feet

this enchanted island
has been invaded by cobras
pythons & boa constrictors
squeezing the life out of my body
through decades of corruption

& some stand here complacent
to be statehood enthusiasts
manipulated by state propaganda
suffering from systematic exclusion

& la bandera waves below old glory
handcuff the future
corporatize the past
control the economics
corporatize the future
control the cattle & crops
colonize the farmer
there are bleeding
jibaros[6] in cayey[7]
there are bleeding
jibaros in guánica[8]
there are bleeding
jibaros in loiza[9]

arm them to defend themselves
before they're brought
to their knees to sing
the star spangled banner.

# FIRST NIGHT IN SANTURCE

my first night here in santurce[10]
i was looking for ghosts
scattered across the barrio obrero

i am trying to find questions
that these dark roads, street lights &
bridges might be able to answer

i find heads under
these new houses
their eyes have been
pulled out & their mouths
have been sowed shut

el viejo on the corner tells me
there are no ghosts here
thats he's been in
the same exact spot forever
i give him two dollars
para dos cervezas

but i can tell they're ghosts here
i can see the transparency
of their memory
the prints of their feet
they carried different
last names than i but
their exit scripts are the same

i stopped visiting
this place long time ago
never felt comfortable enough
& those who are still here
live in dilapidated houses
with pictures of dead family
members hanging crooked on the wall

their framed eyes move
when i walk by
i look at the frames from
the side & they tell me
there are no ghosts here
but i can see the plasma
on the flickering light poles
like a fading optimism

i am standing in
the middle of the street
in the middle of the night
watching the ghosts run around
with no pain in their bones
no more worries about debt
no more worries about sickness
no more worries about tomorrow

& they laugh so loud in the night
they sound like the wind

they tell me there
are no ghosts here.

# THIRTY WAYS OF LOOKING AT A NUYORICAN

I.
i do not wake up
to roosters, i wake up
to construction sights
& exhaling buses

II.
english was fed to me
by my television baby sitter

III.
i barely know
what oceans & beaches look like
orchard beach & brighton beach
do not count

IV.
i know how to grow culture
but don't know how to grow food
i buy rice in bags, beans in cans
& piraguas in union square

V.
my skin is pale, my cousin's skin is black
we are called white boy & negro
at the same time on the same table

VI.
i do not know how to hotwire a car
i don't even know how to drive

VII.
i have a fear of needles, so being a junkie
was never a consideration but being a thief
(sometimes)

VIII.
i have a library of dead heroes
that i have stolen

IX.
as i remember it
i've been called jewish
more times after i turned
twenty-one for whatever reason

X.
i do not believe in haircuts
until i cut my hair again

XI.
when riding the train
everyone can be nuyorican[11]
but most are new yorkers

XII.
i always get lost in queens

XIII.
i've walked into a riot once
& immediately walked out

XIV.
excelsior

XV.
in my house pictures of albizu campos,[12]
jimi hendrix, che guevara, the beatles
& jesus christ hang next to each other

XVI.
people make fun of me for not knowing
how to drive then they visit new york city
& completely understand why

XVII.
police have stopped me
for looking too out of place
i was standing in front of my building

XVIII.
when in london searching
for a puerto rican flag is trying
to find a needle in a brick wall

XIX.
nuyoricans dance in their sleep

XX.
spanish does not make you nuyorican
english does not make you nuyorican

XXI.
pedro, papoleto, miguel, tato,
sandra, louis, jorge, algarin & bimbo[13]
walk into a bar & performed magic
performed beautiful magic

XXII.
my obituary is not written yet

XXIII.
when i returned to puerto rico
everyone stared at me then i spoke
i think it was my accent

XXIV.
my son was born in chicago
lived in harlem
lives to michigan
is puerto rican & irish
& i keep his heart
in the bronx

XXV.
nuyoricans look like everyone
nuyoricans look like no one

XXVI.
i'm like every puerto rican you know
i'm not like every puerto rican you know

XXVII.
in the middle of the bandera
is the heart of a nuyorican
ask betances[14]

XXVIII.
el morro is more famous
than the empire state building

XXIX.
a nuyorican & a puerto rican
walk into the bar & they both
ask for a cuba libre

XXX.
patria. sangre. libertad.

## PLAYA SUCIA TO EL LOCAL

i was there

watching the
water splash
against the walls
of cabo rojo[15]
that fall into
the caribbean sea
displaying a new
set of sea foam colors
every season
jose tells me
stories that
i would have
never known

i stand in front of
el faro de los morrillos[16]
i stare at it intensely
i memorize how it stands
majestically with its eyes
wide open overlooking the sea
it tells me it finds travelers
before they arrive to warn them
of the colonialism here
of the corruption here

el faro shines bright
shows a path to help
travelers navigate through
the mona passage[17]
el faro tells travelers
to be weary with what
they decide to do because
the government here
will not shine a light

el faro warns them
to be careful because
the border patrol is ruthless

i was there

climbing down
the rocky terrain
from el faro
grappling on
to the limestone
to keep me from
a 200 foot drop
i pray i don't fall
& have my face
ripped apart by
boulders & earth
made shrapnel

i see the ocean
i am happy to be
in these waters of playa sucia
with sea weed entangled
in my hair & i rise out
i smell the salt
i taste the water
the rocks are clipping my feet
but i don't care
the sea healed me

i was there

with urayoán noel
at a bar talking about poetry
& personal histories
from the boogie down
to rio piedras[18]
watching bands noodle

around on stage while
the crowd is happy to see
their friends imagine
that they've made it

urayoán & i repeat
the word borracho
then we bump into
yarimir of mima
in the street playing
with other musicians
we go to another bar
where we talk about music
all the while hundreds of
teenage puertooriqueños
are having their first beer
first kiss, first bomba
first rock show & wake up
to their first hangover

i was there

on fernandez juncos
at the first queer rock
show at el local[19]
i drank medalla
like it was water
i wrote on the walls
while the bands played
& wore their love for
the misfits & los angeles punk
yarimir was there
urayoán was there
& a friend of his jose miguel
who volunteered to drive me home
at the end of the night
he was inebriated to say the least
as he swirled around the streets

like an erratic dolphin
he started tailgating a cop car
that also seemed drunk
& after almost driving over
a cliff into the caribbean sea
we somehow made it to where
i was staying in one piece

the next day
i went back
to el local to see
the writings on the wall
it said

i was there.

## WAITING AT THE BUS STOP
## IN SAN JUAN

i know i should've went home
when everyone else left
i remember i said it with ease
"oh i'll take the bus back"
& my friends looked at me
like i was crazy
are you sure? they asked
yeah i'll be fine

so now i'm here on
a long dark street
in san juan[20]
waiting for the bus
to take me back home
buses are the worst here
by the way

i don't know how to drive
new york city has made it easy
for me not to care for it
& because i'm usually too cheap
or broke to pay for a cab

the night's air is humid
with a sky full of stars
no one's outside tonight
i am standing in the middle
of the street trying to take a photo

i am trying to figure out
when the next bus is coming
but technology is useless on
a monday night past 1am

its quiet out here, real quiet

i can actually hear myself think
new york city is only this quiet
on a wednesday at 4am

i left la respuesta[21]
which velcro had the place jumping
which is why i always want to stay
so i can get everything from the night
the sweat, the rhythm & the bass

when i leave i walk up fernandez juncos
reading the street names
san jorge, jordan
& i stop at avenida boriquen

i walk into the ~~walgreens~~
that's open 24 hours
to get snacks, some soda
& the girl behind the register
asks me how my night was?
   told her it was great
did you go to la respuesta?
   yes i did
you're lucky she said
i'm stuck here working

i tell her not to worry
about what has passed
but what will come tomorrow
i ramble about saving money
& big dreams but i cant recall most of it

she asks where i'm from
i tell her i'm puerto rican
& i gave her the usual rundown
born in new york city
lived in levittown
moved back to new york city

lived there most of my life
now reacquainting myself
with the island

she laughs says
i speak spanish funny
but likes that i try
i ask her about the bus
& how frequent it runs
la wahwah?! she laughs again
says i'll be waiting until 6am
for the next one

i walking around trying to figure
out my next move & then i see
the bus pulling in half a block away
& then i do what everyone dreads
i run for it

& i'm hoping the bus driver sees me
& that he still has some sense
of humanity knowing how late it is
& i'm running fast
wally west/barry allen fast[22]

my head's shaking from
all the alcohol in my system
i drop my snack &
say goodbye to it
      but i made it
      barely, but made it
      i turn around & look back
      at ~~walgreens~~ & the register girl
      is at the corner waving at me
      i wave back, get on board, sit down
      breathe & look out the window
      to see this beautiful town at 2am
      at 35 miles an hour.

# REMEMBER

we were very tired
we've been fighting all year
camped out at various places
our friends are still in jail & they
shot our cousin last week at a protest
we have one useless governor after another
that sold the beaches to ibm & coca cola
& closed 300 schools all over the island
we were distraught & hungry
we ate an apple an day
sometimes even an orange
it was bright, smelled like a trap
& two of our friends passed out
from the heat

the sky was full of kites
the ocean breeze could
knock a person down
& the sun rose dripping gold

we had almost no fight left in us
then we saw someone reading
*no* by jose de diego[23]
& understood that this fight
has gone through generations

     a child runs up & tells our friend
"i want to be you when i grow up"
& they respond that there is no glory
in fighting for liberation unless the island
is free, & in that process most of us will
be arrested, exiled & killed
     the child runs away crying

our friend looks at us & says
that's how i feel everyday.

## ON THE LAST DAY

the last day will be
a glorious one
filled with things
that i love like spend
time with my son
read my favorite poems
listen to music
the whole day
dance with my mother
who hates dancing
tell my sister i love her
& that i'm proud of her
call everyone
i've cared about
& i thank them
for the years
of friendship
i tell people
on the street
that they're
beautiful & that
compliment is free
ride a train
ride a bike
ride a boat
go to the
tallest building
& scream beautiful
things like i love you
& maybe someone
will respond
i'll fight for my
independence
& paint murals
of my heroes
across my heart

betances, neruda,
albizu, che, king,
kahlo, dali, miro,
miles, malcolm, lorca
de burgos, nin,
lennon, hendrix,
bolivar, marti,
hostos, toussaint,
zapata, zappa,
baraka, ginsberg,
jaco, coltrane,
cobain, basquiat,
& garcia marquez[23]
& i thank them
for their art &
i've learned how to
live on my feet
& fly in my dreams
& i only kneel
when i feel thankful
& i talk to the universe
when i feel no one is listening
& i apologize to those
i should apologize to
& the rest i learned that
they're still not not worthy
i speak to my father
who's been dead for years
& it's not the first time
but i tell him about my trips
to puerto rico & how i think
he would've been proud

i revisit
all the catalysts
of my life
& i remember
& reenact them

& see the young
versions of myself
wild, stupid
rambunctious
ego driven
hyper-sugared
up all night
graffiti sprayed
& broadway made
& i write my name
to honor the past
& i thank those
moments for being
a foundational block
for right now & i think
of all the cities &
countries i've visited
puerto rico, cuba
london, st. john
amsterdam, brussels
barcelona, toronto
los angeles, versailles
washington d.c., chicago
detroit, montreal
calexico, philadelphia
oakland, albuquerque
atlantic city, sacramento
st. thomas, miami
san diego, brixton
berkeley, providence
tortola, virgin gorda
rotterdam, manchester
boston, berlin, rome
paris & san francisco
& then i visit
all the houses
my son has lived in
& i thank them

for keeping him safe
then i take a walk
around the city
that i love & hate
& i eat pizza from
patsy's in spanish harlem
drink sangria from
camaradas el barrio[24]
& then i go home
to the only place
i've ever considered home
on the grand concourse
with memories in
every splice of
hardwood floor
i bring down
the paintings
pack up the books
put the guitars away
sweep the living room
& open my old black chest
that has all the journals
i've ever written in
& i take them out
to see how erratic
my handwriting was
& someone once
said it looks like
a sociopath's handwriting
but i've never believed
in a diagnosis given
by a doctor
who was paid
by medicaid
then i read
the first poem
i wrote
it was called

LIFE
& i read to myself
& see how ironic it was
that this 17 year old
was trying to tackle
something so massive
as LIFE
but i don't blame him
he had nothing then
he probably thought
he would never
achieve anything
go anywhere
be anyone
love anything
love anyone
or be loved
& i see the progression
through the years
& then i go to
my bedroom window
the one that my son
& i have both
looked out of
& i look at the big sky
across the street
over the abandoned church
& i watch the sunset
& if today is
my last day i'll say
      damn!
      i was a lucky
      bastard wasn't
      i.

# HOME IS THE FLOWER OF THE LAND

tierra is the first word
the island teaches us

the wind is our navigator through
this land of the valiant lord

the coasts are crystalline cobalt blue
& we give all the hurricanes names

these pueblos of deserts & jungles
opens the roads to the edge of history

we are measured in size & location
harmonize in a minor key

we carry exoduses on our backs
our blood is a lineage of café y caña

we've built columns of smoke
to obscure the clarity of this gorgeous sky

seventy eight provinces from end to end
from faro to faro, from la mar to el oceano

we've erected gigantic billboards of
foreign products, molasses & gasoline

electric lines cover the island like sheet music
the city's technical progress has invaded the countryside

we torture the muscles of these mountains
these small towns are being reconstructed

transformed by irrigation radio waves
& the smart phones, we've increased

the speed of development on our backs & legs
tomorrow seems like a frightening place

of radioactive beaches, plastic forests
towns of hydraulic energy & neon mountain sides

the exploding super-population hasn't culturally
developed the next generation

we have to defend the island from the ivory
statues that represent an oppressive future

we cannot assure ourselves the air
we breathe will always be free

we cannot assure that these homes of ours
will always belong to us & not to a bank of leeches

the geographic position of our land
has determined the course of our history

we are a forced collective personality
we are casualties of imperialism

fastened in between two americas
we lack volume, we lack ports

our island can be seen in two days
tourism is the mirrored ball & chain

we are an empty shells of our former glory
a narrow house cramped by the plains & valleys

the immediate expansion of our landscape
is a traumatic result due to the invasion

if we stretch our bodies far enough
we can touch the four corners

our history would have been different
if our land was different

our heroes & fighters who did not fit in
who fled & died in foreign lands

may have been treated different because
they would've had more space to create

we are geological positioning
we are invigorating climates

we are biological constitutions
we are imperial landscapes

we are trapped in a perpetual cycle of self destruction
operating on our collective psychosis

we were once woods, pastures,
swamps & untapped potential

now we're a paradise in a schizophrenic conundrum
divided by invisible titles of state & independence

we are jibaros with satellite dishes
we are farmers who carry computers

we are fast food, fast highways,
corporate tools, monopolizing landlords

our hearts sit on the lap of rediscovery
our hands balance the conflict & cooperation

home is the flower of the land
caribbean & atlantic picturesque

our expression is coupled with
our anguish of yearning for freedom

our memories are made of wood, metal
history, music, poetry, folklore, & tradition

this century has been a long fight
& search for our self defining roles

these coasts are crystalline cobalt blue
we give all the hurricanes names

the wind is our navigator through
this land of the valiant lord

libertad is the first word
we taught ourselves

tierra is the first word
the island taught us.

# EL YUNQUE

no one ever
tells you the
actual journey
it takes to get
to las cascadas
de el yunque
from san juan

the highway
was built to arrive
faster than before
but no one ever
tells you about
being stuck at
a toll booth in
the hot sun
behind a makeshift
horse cart
being pulled by
a old ford explorer

& no one ever
tells you while
you're on the highway
you'll see these
massive signs saying

EL YUNQUE NATIONAL FOREST[25]

but then when
you arrive
in rio grande
all you'll see
are small signs
that points
in the direction

of the mountain
& it can be easily
missed then after
the u-turns &
the drive up on
the curves &
after you pass
the entrance
you'll search
for parking
which will take
you a mile
further up
the anvil
only then
can you
actually say
you've arrived
at el yunque

& no one ever
tells you about
the rigorous walk
hike, climb, through
the rainforest

& no one ever
tells you how far it is
everyone will say
"oh, como cinco minutos"

& you'll continue
to walk up & down
across & over
for at least another
thirty minutes
feeling like
an explorer

walking past
people at a pace
that will even
surprise you

then when you
finally arrive
you'll see this
beautiful majestic sight
of las cascadas de el yunque
aqui en borinquen/boriken[26]

& no one will tell you
how incredibly cold
the water is

& no one will tell you
how you'll never
want to leave
how you'll want
to live in a tent
or in a cave but
you'll know getting
food will be pretty hard

no one will tell you
when you leave
how magical you'll feel
how amazing the
whole journey was

hope no one ever
tells you the whole
experience because
then you might

think it's not
worth the trip.

## INSIDE THE MUSEUM OF NATURAL HISTORY

on his hot summer day
so my son & i
go to the museum
because a museum
is the only logical choice
when there are
no good movies showing
& your apartment has
no air conditioning

we give .50 cents
to the museum
because the tourists
behind me are going
paying the full price
of $25 dollars
& probably those
behind them too
i give the cashier
the don't give me that look
of not paying the full price
we pay new york state taxes
you've gotten enough
money out of us through
the years

depending on which
entrance you choose
the museum is a majestic moment
but we entered through
the 81st street train station
& it's very anti-climatic
with a security guard
yelling at everyone to
stay on the left in a straight line

we walk in, stare at the directory
i ask him, where do you want to start?
he points at the top floor of dinosaurs
something he's been obsessed with since
he was a toddler

we get in the elevator
we head to the top
so we can work our way down

we are explorers searching
for tyrannosaurus rex's & ancestors
of domesticated animals

my son's eyes are wide open
the enormity of these creatures
no one has ever seen in person

i love the museum
more than most people
but the museum of natural history
is a survival strategy game
an obstacle course of
who can get out of the way faster
& say excuse me less times
when trying to navigate
through the these aisles

we work our way through
with of 27 excuse me's
& 44 collisions by people
who aren't watching where they walk

a grown man bumps into my son
he turns around & shrugs it off
like it was my son's fault
i give him a death stare
that burns a hole in his skull

he sees me & apologizes
i told him to apologize
to my son not to me

we journeyed through
          rural america but not actual america
          biodiversity but not cultural diversity
          environmental halls but no mention of
          environmental climate change
          human origin & fossils but
          not current human conflict
          reptiles & amphibians like snakes in capitol hill
          primitive mammals like republicans
          invertebrates & phylum creatures like politicians
          ocean life but not oceanic corporate destruction
          birds, birds, & more birds but not nyc pigeons
          africa & rare gems but no words
          on blood diamonds from slavery & colonization
          mexico & the celebration of its culture
          but no mention of the horrors of the current
          immigration laws or stealing of the land, the forced
          immigration or invisible borders
          central america but no write up on the coups
          funded by the united states the last 50 years
          mammals, mammals, mammals of every kind
          even meteorites that have fallen from the sky
          because those are so f*cking important
          we saw north american forests
          pacific indians, plains indians
          woodland indians, northwest coast indians
          south american peoples because the word
          indigenous may have been too long
          but no mention of the destruction of the amazon
          forest because the same corporations trying to destroy
          them are the ones funding these exhibits
          north american mammals not including
          donkeys & elephants & we both loved the big blue
          whale in the middle of the large room

my son asked me so many questions
& i answered them the best i could

i tell him one day
you my young little animal liberationist
will make your own decisions

& you will look at these institutions
that may not include any of us
until we are dead
thats when all the things
i tell you will make sense

why fast food pizza cost more
than a cup of celery or why people
look at you strange for donating
to dog shelters

you'll see how this world
will work against you
remember your principles
& remember to look up
once in a blue because

one day
a meteor will fall
out the sky & i want you
to be ready because everyone else
will have their heads in their devices
& you'll yell at them to run to safety

but being
the primitive mammals
that they are
they'll stand around
get wiped out & eventually
end up in a museum.

## SATURDAY NIGHT IN VIEJO SAN JUAN

when you stare at
el morro at night
you'll notice two things
how massive the night is
when there's no lights
& how many people are looking
for an adventure in the dark

im wandering around
viejo san juan[27]
& depending who you ask
i either look like a new tourist
or a seasoned local
i observe all the boriquas[28]
& tourists looking for love
in one night stands
a moment that can
mean everything
or a memory that can make
life feel worthy or destroy it

each street has music sidewinding
with switchblades dance partners
& i always look down while
i'm walking to avoiding stepping
on a accident waiting to happen

the cobble stone
is a melody of yesterday
holding on to last night
the houses are vibrant
but this is no different
than the east village
with a million bars
trying to make their

rent off a weekend of
high school & college kids
wasting their money
on another saturday night
in viejo san juan

i walk into nuyorican café
on calle san francisco
there's no poets here
that i can see but i could be wrong
it's salsa saturday
i pick a corner
watch as men
& women dance
defy gravity

i leave the bar
& wander through
the narrow streets
looking for a secret
i left there ten years before
the sun is creeping
the streets are empty
i walked every street
from calle de luna
to paseo de la princesa
to calle norzagaray
i never found the secret
i went back to el morro
& a cafecito y pan
& the sun is running
all over the great lawn
the ocean is brilliant

but the darkness that
consumed el morro
last night will never
leave the black of my eyes.

# THE BLACK MORNING

bandera negra de la mañana
we drink you with
ash & saltwater
feed children sand
when they cry hungry

en la plaza de viejo san juan
you can smell the ocean
ay un mujer who feeds pigeons
at noon & recites *la boriqueña*[29]
you can cut the apathy of
this island with a butter knife

bandera negra de la tarde
we eat you with flat beer
& stale white bread
our bellies are fed frustration
we vomit the institutions
the united states gave us
fifty years ago

there's a man that walks
around with a sign that says
      "libertad or muerte"
he trips on the cobblestone
& his sign breaks
this is a sign of our liberation
this is a metaphor
not everyone will understand

he lays on the street
& people try to help him up
he screams:
      "help the island! alluda la isla"
they leave him on the floor
until the police arrive

bandera negra de la noche
we role play freedom
like imagination, like theatre
we don't know
what freedom tastes like
we don't know
what freedom smells like

we are generations
of imperialist bastards
we tug on it's hair
love its breath
eat their face
bear their children
but we purge & urge
rebuke & puke
& die & die
a million times over
to populate these landfills

we role plays
with hoods on
carry toys that
sound like thunder
smack lightning
from our knuckles
take the surnames of the villains
who killed our parents

we have a love affair with life
because we can't see freedom
from this angle of detachment
we burn our skin to feel
rip our flesh to see our blood
we hope its the color of anger
cardinal, vermillion
any scarlet pigment
falling from the sky

but it's not it's white
the whitest night the world
has ever produced
white like imperialism
white like cotton
white like political ballots

we break into the box
they locked freedom in
& escape during the night
with the stars shining on our backs

we paint our flag black to show
our resistance has a symbol
our black flag of resistance

we wave it above
the statues of dead presidents
we wave it in front of the corporations
that only think of the island as an investment
we wave it in front of the police officers
that kidnap us in plain clothing
we wave it at state capitals
to save public education
we wave it with our bloody hands
& broken bodies

we'll wave it until
puerto rico is free.

# LOS MUÑECOS

howdy doody[30]
is starring at the playhouse
& the politicians
in puerto rico
are the opening act

they strangle themselves
with the strings that control
them so they can be seen
by the corporate marionettist
but they operate behind the curtain
the audience applauds
when the sign lights up
they audience doesn't see
how they've marionetted
our liberation & freedom

the politicians laugh
in the show they star in
because government is theatre
the cameras are rolling
they pump their fist
name streets after dead revolutionaries
declare holidays on their death date
erect statues of the colonizer
the audience applauds
when the sigh lights up

they are trying to destroy
the future of the next generation
call it progress
call it a promise
call them muñecos
call them maniquí
their strings are pulled right
they sell off the island

& close the hospitals
their strings are pulled left
& they close the schools
& sell off their pride

the spotlight is bright
they each have a solo
to entertain the corporate heads

do not believe in
the puppets in power
they enjoy the strings
controlling them
gives them purpose
they believe their act will be
seen by the marionettist
& that their show will air
on prime time right after
the evening news

      (applause)
      (scene)
      (end).

## LESSONS ON A PARK BENCH
## IN RIO PIEDRAS

I.
at high noon
when the sun
is most unforgiving
sit split in
the shade
to experience
both sensations
hold a cup of café
& a cold cerveza
think about
living in
a colony
how the
constant
rage when
pondering
what self
sufficiency
looks like
think about
analogies
you tell
yourself
to make
thing more
acceptable
but a balance
of oppression
is only brought
about by
liberation
this is what
rattles your
brain at a

quick meal
across the
street from
the university
of puerto rico
de rio piedras
you see protests
the rallies
the look of
frustration
on their faces
when all they
want is their
future to arrive
with no barricades
no obstacles
they were innocent
bystanders before today
then they were caught in
the hurricane of decisions
made by a government
who don't care
about them or
their future
they ask their parents
& receive roundabout
answers about patria
capitalism, that the
government knows best
& it is what it is
& they don't accept
it as an answer
they are not vago,
impreciso, incierto,
or vagabundo
they are not that
they are so much
more than that

II.
i hear bad brains[31]
playing in a bar
across the street
there are viejos
professors
& freshman
all drinking
cerveza &
eating rice & beans
i stare at the
body language
watch the body
movements
see who's
breaking hearts
who's telling
their lover
that they
are forever
who's plotting
a revolt in the laundromat
they're trying to
cleans the sins
from the night before
but a new night is coming
one full of possibility
a whole new night
of new introductions
pleasure to meet you's
i hear the routines
& buy a drink then
air guitar to led zeppelin[32]
drum solo to rock & roll
sing the night away
the way Cedric does
in at the drive-in[33]
or the mars volta[34]

three six packs later
four conversations
of political theory
& liberation practices
& the bar smells like
a thursday afternoon
& a saturday night
at the same time
i drink in the street
making the small roads
of rio piedras look huge
it's swarming with
everything from
clergymen to doctors
dancers to phd candidates
i do a head count
on the main road
& then they disappear
into their homes
cars, taxis, bikes
only to return
tomorrow
earlier than today
to continue their
conversations
of everything
& anything
with a plate of
rice & beans
& a nice cold
cerverza.

# EASTER SUNDAY IN MAYAGÜEZ

i am eating a sandwich
at ricomimi in mayagüez
it's easter sunday
talib kweli[35]& common[36]
are on the television

rumor has it someone
was resurrected today
but i've never seen it
happen with my own eyes
& i know a lot of good
people who've passed away

were they messiahs? no
but just because a book
tells me one was doesn't
mean any of it is true

common has a song
called resurrection
back when he carried sense
      & today i watched a procession
      walk up the street &
      after they were gone
      there was still fake blood
      on the sidewalk

people are reenacting
something that
possibly happened
over 2,000 years ago
in the middle east
with a religion that was
used to oppress with a statue
of a man that does not
resemble the deceased

i am eating a glazed donut
waiting for an elderly couple
to move from my usual seat

everyone looks at me
like they know i'm not from mayagüez[37]
i am used to receiving looks
i am comfortable with my donut

people are wearing
their sunday's best
their resurrection best
a lot of white with
no purity in sight
don't really care
for these morals
that have been
generationally
engraved into us
they're patriarchal
white supremacist
hand me downs
psychological constructs
used to hate ourselves

two cops walk in & in puerto rico
cops always look like they're in a movie
dressed up with vests & guns
looking like they could blow the head
off any person claiming to be the messiah

whenever i about to eat a meal
people look at me
& say *buen provecho*[38]
& i know my face is giving them
a look letting them know
i'm not from around here
i don't think they're used to that

i say gracias in response

i'm still waiting for my usual seat
the elderly couple looks like
they're never going to leave
they keep eating & eating
there's sunday mass
on the television now
it's easter sunday
i leave the ricomimi
with my unfinished
sandwich at the table

letting everyone know
i'm not from around here.

# THE ADVENTURES OF LEFTY

I. *Miguel & The Ocean*

i pour my father's ashes
into the ocean
i am drowning in
i feel the thunder
shake me alive
from the infinite deep
it's the closest
we've been in years

i was saved
because a hurricane
pushed me to shore
a face full of sand
& apologies to my father
who i avoided like raindrops
& now i'm here drenched
i stare at the sky
see his evaporated
ashes become rain
i feel his downpour
i feel the anguish
of the bad hand dealt

i stand in the rain
fully accepting & holding
myself accountable
for my decisions with him
i walk to el puente en santurce
that crosses into rio piedras
i see him running across the street
chasing elegies & gathering scars
like currency, i see his blood on
the corners of these makeshift houses
with metal roofs that sing when it rains

it does not wash his blood away

i see his face in a cloud
i know he's been following me
i write his name miguel
at the foot of the bridge

& a little boy walks up to me
he looked like us when we were
little boys, he asks me
        ¿quién fue miguel?
        el fue un hombre hermoso,
        un hombre brillante,
        que tuvo una vida dura.

he puts his hand
on my shoulder & says
        "mira, una cara en la nube!"

yesterday i was in puerto rico
& i left my father there.

II. *Miguel & The Constellation*

above the bodega
on the grand concourse
where the robbery happened
above the delivery boy's bike
where he rides miles of experience
above the smells of mofongo in
the mornings that sound like the fania all-stars[39]
above the legally abandoned building
by the city, who still have a few families in it
a boy stares out the window
counting the stars
gives them names
of his dead friends
says they'll live forever now

his eyes constellation bright
wears a shazam[40] t-shirt
because he loves lightning bolts
& is proud to knows his name means
solomon, hercules atlas,
zeus, achilles, & mercury[41]

when he was young
he wanted to be an astronaut
but he was told no puerto rican kid
could ever be an astronaut
they told him
  miguel can't go into space!
  angel can't go into space!
  why? why not me?
no one ever answered him

he goes to the rooftop
& screams at the top of his lungs
  why not me!
  why not me!

& the sky start sparkling
the stars move closer together
the electrons are
dancing off his face
  why not me?

he whispers & stands on the ledge
& says wisdom, strength, stamina
power, courage, speed
then he levitates
higher & higher & higher
until he starts yelling
"i'm an astronaut!!!!"
& *shazam*!

he disappears.

III. *Miguel & The Fruit*

the day is a bruised fruit
with dark spots all over
the divide is stark
it's an abandoned harvest
in puerto rico from san juan to ponce
the high noon feel like a noose

the oceans, seas & rivers are boiling
the beautiful water is blistering my hands
i am trying to hold up my patria & i get burned

living on this island
is a metaphor for division

politicians are like crows, they peck &
yell that it's all theirs, everything is theirs
from the mangos that fall in abuela's backyard
to the sugar the coffee & the beaches

they sell everything here, the seashells & the sand
they even look for oil here
it's in their programming to plunder
& we've been plundered
for over a hundred years

we grow produce here
then they take our produce
send it to florida then sell it back
to us weeks later
our once fresh fruit now
has american worms
crawling out of it
but even with sofrito
colonization doesn't taste good
their bullets, bombs, boats,
ballots, & bureaucracy

can't be seasoned so it can have flavor
they try to make it digestible
but you can't disguise
oppression with spices.

IV. *Miguel & The Hurricane*

every other season
i deal with hurricanes
all of them carrying names
of deceased friends & old lovers

the worst ones are
always named
after my mother
she rips everything apart
nothing is ever good enough
no one is ever good enough
she stands above me
like a force of nature

i stands there
no matter how old
i actually am
i am a insecure boy
hoping she accept me
that she'll like who i brings home
who i love, hoping that
she keep her racism out
of her mouth & away from
my lover's ears

she never liked the trigeñita
i dated, had children with
a woman who arms
i eventually lived in
& called home
& my hurricane of a mother

who tried to destroy this house
barely even acknowledged it
would turn her back to it
never call the house by name
left the room when the mother
of my children entered
& would never acknowledge her
would stay by the a window
until she left

i was always amazed
how she was able to destroy
things without even looking at it

V. *Miguel & The Blackout*

summer of 1977
i found himself in harlem
with only a knife & these hands
while the city was burning
from the ground up

i had to walk back to the bronx
it's not a long walk but this city
is blacked out & crazy so
i had to be a little cautious

i walk from lenox ave. to first avenue
then cross the willis ave. bridge
no need for expose the metal

i complained about electric company
all the way home
& i had to get home
to my pregnant trigeñita,
& my 6 year old daughter
when i got to the middle
of the bridge

i turned around
looked at both boroughs
& saw them both of fire

the world is going mad
& i kept walking
i saw the bronx loot itself dry
we know the term
i don't have to repeat
but these landlords have been
doing that for a long time
for insurance money

the city was already on high alert
because the son of sam
was out here murdering people

the city was broke
mayor beane was joke
when people ask
where were you when the lights went out?

i tell them, i was on a bridge
it was so hot that day
a typical new york july heatwave
where if you lived by coney island
all you did was stay on the beach

i finally got home
& we stared out the window
i wanted to go out
but i remember the black out of 1965
& i got arrested for trying to take a television
so now since there was no electricity
the window became news & entertainment
channel 2 stayed on the air
& the riots & looting continued
& i watched everything

the next day
there was still no electricity
i heard they stole fifty cars
from a dealer
        man
          i would've loved
          a new car

they called the blackout
an act of god
& i don't disagree with them
not after what i saw that night

VI. *Miguel & The New York Yankees*

before women
my first love was baseball
i grew up less than a mile
from the house that ruth built

i always wanted to play rightfield
like my idol roberto clemente[42]
a puerto rican with a cannon for an arm
played for the pittsburgh pirates
every puerto rican kid
wanted to be clemente
& every puerto rican in new york
wanted clemente to be a yankee

i wanted to be that player in right field
if the yankees never got clemente
to play next to mickey mantle
& wear number 21

one day, i tore his achilles
running in a game of daredevil
jumping over pot holes
& eventually landed in one

that summer was a window
& stoop season
no chasing sunsets
no catching clouds
no creating melodies
with my feet

i just sat & watched
the heat dance off the concrete
i lost the desire to play that summer
still watched every game that season
still dreamt of right field
still went to yankee games

but i couldn't catch up
to the curve balls being
thrown at me.

# SQUEEZING THROUGH A NEEDLE POINT

baby boy
toddler
big boy
mamas boy
little man
boriqua
little man
mamas boy
hijo
hermano
school boy
big ears
dumbo
class clown
r-o-j-a-s (roe-jazz)
hyper kid
troubled student
adhd student
foreigner
gringo
que soy?
fela's son
lefty's kid
tina's brother
new yorker
truant
high school freshman
troubled teenager
teenager
young man
club head
village head
delinquent
graffiti writer
burke

typical city kid
funk super hero
graffiti writer
criminal
hooligan
hoodlum
criminal
cabron
high school drop out
little brother
rock & roller
hip hop head
zulu nation
black panther[43]
young lord[44]
boriqua
nationalista
independista
mujeriego
scatterbrained
taxpayer
inventer
boriqua
writer
r-o-j-a-s (roe-jazz)
poet
afro
bonafide
graffiti writer
poet
performer
egotistical
activist
nuyorican
blanquito
bronxite
teacher
wanderluster

new father
little brother
mamas boy
teacher
energetic
afro poetic
long hair
curly hair
guitarist
mona passage
musician
heartbreaker
heartbroken
rebuilder
insecure
secure
lazy
hard work
social butterfly
recluse
older
reserved
performer
reserved
friend
boriqua
new yorker
puerto rican
nuyorican
fela's son
lefty's kid
tina's brother
john's father
poet
bonafide
r-o-j-a-s (roe-haus).

## AT THE GATES

the gates are bordered up
the signs are bi-lingual
the school is practically empty

a lot of parking spaces available now
there's desks mounted on top of each other
the imaginary debt is quicksand for this island

los viejos turn their nose up on them
call them spoiled brats sin vergüenza
there's tents visible through out the campus

living on schools grounds to defend
the concept that education is a right
for everyone & should not be dismantled

by exploiting politicians who cripple
a country & then are hired to fix the
problem they created, thats an oxymoron

yesterday there was a protest
at the capitol building in san juan
there were thousands of puertorriqueños

with signs that say "se acabó, las promesas"
wearing black flag t'shirts with their children
on their arm, whole communities marching

& fighting against corruption & the police
dressed in riot gear from head to toe
stand in line, helmets down, raise their arms

& spray their colonialism on the future.

# LESSONS ON A PARK BENCH
# IN LOISAIDA

I.
i've learned to be
quiet in loud spaces
to be still in
room full of
manics, to be
completely calm
when chaos in
happening
learn to make
decisions for
happiness, it
won't be easy but
no one said finding
happiness was
going to be
learn to enjoy
laughing hard
from the gut
be honest with self
& the decisions made
would take some back
even say we'll regret some
learn to not tell people
everything anymore
especially in poems
in conversations
seen them used in
the wrong context
used against in
arguments
& i'll stare
dumbfounded
at that act then
realize i have to

make more decisions
to keep myself happy
i've lived many lives
& loved many people
may not love them now
but i loved them once
i used to always be with
a group of people
now i learned to
be reclusive
another word for
self preservation
humbled that
i'm still here
that i still create
thought everything
would've folded up
cut my hair off
get a regular job
like everyone who
didn't know me told me
don't know why
they all look miserable
i learned to love myself
some days are harder than
others but i'm patient with that
don't tell people of the process
it's one i've kept sacred
some days are harder than others
some days are harder than others
i repeat it
i'm aware of how good
the good days are
how wonderful
the wonderful days are
life is about repetition, right?
i learned that when
i woke up in the morning

i kept my body quiet
looked in the mirror
& saw myself growing
aging right
before my eyes
saw the years
in my skin
checked if i could
still see the wild child inside
i love learning & exploring
i love sitting on
benches in loisaida[45]
on avenue c.
watching everything
i love being able
to still do the things i love
i said these things before
but i need reminders too
i learned that
love is hard work
& hard work
is a beautiful thing
i put effort into it
i'm consistent & punctual
that's what love is
a beautiful thing
& i failed at love
many times but never
for lack of trying
i failed at many things
but never for lack of trying
some days are
harder than others
but some days
are easier than others
some days are lovely
& i deserve those
yes i do.

II.
when i desire someone
i know that everything
i know will be tested
destroyed, obliterated
reconstructed & reconfigured
i will do things i thought
i never would do
knowing that a no
could prevent progress
so i say yes sometimes
even if means eating
something i'm allergic too
do you eat shrimp?
knowing what will happen
immediately after
but a yes allows for growth
for possibility &
taking chances in
the name of desire
in the name of affection
in the name of love
is understandable
but i don't risk
my happiness
taking risks in
the way i let
people speak to me
or don't value me
in the way i want to be
when i'm with someone
i ask people questions
that i really want to hear
answers for & it's okay
if someone doesn't like
kendrick lamar,[46] pj harvey[47]
stevie wonder,[48] or radiohead[49]
so i show them why they should

show them how their
DNA can be changed
if they allow it

i tell them how sitting
on a bench in loisaida
while reading
willie perdomo,[50] patricia smith[51]
lucille clifton,[52] aracelis girmay[53]
tony medina[54] & jason reynolds[55]
changed my perspective
changed my whole life
so i give thanks
& feed all the pigeons
regardless what
the sign says.

## JOHN PABLO ROJAS IS A COMET CRASHING OUT THE SKY

i stand among the dead flock of birds, shaped in v formation at grand army plaza, atop of the weeds in the concrete, in the packed streets of times square, in the south south bronx, he came crashing out the sky

beneath the streets, beneath woodlawn cemetery, beneath the pigeons, beneath the sky scraping towers of capitalism, farther down among forgotten demigods, formally elected officials & washed up rookie baseball players

staring into the black, beyond street & block, beyond bridge & river, beyond fire & time, beyond the borough & island, beyond friends & family, beyond cause & effect, beyond religious purification

over genocide & gang banging, corruption & city officials, consumption & consumerism, under developed communities, malnourished imaginations, corporate gentrification versus community salvation

next to the safe deposit banks of safety depending pockets of the poor, next to the dilapidated condos of their tiny dreams, the trust funded education, the greed dripping from their tongues

everyone is trying to leave their immortality in my mouth, inside a centrally parked cemetery in the middle of my skull, they trying to chop my hands off, chop my head off, & buy my body parts, everything is not for sale

among the leaders with blindfolds on, in the man made cities in the skies, with their man made titles of world domination, in the corrupt police precincts, in the very overcrowded jails, in the racist american court system with the organizers, the activists, the drummers, the poets, the painters, the dancers, the rioters, the musicians, the migration, the lawyers, the straphangers, the running lost, the mothers of dead children, the orphaned children

the wind from the gulf of mexico, reminded me of the memory of south america, i see these dragons made of clouds, i see these ships with names of dead generals & i'm supposed to be happy when they say they come in peace & the ocean is dead still

all that i carry is an empty briefcase for possibility, with my heart, my fears, i stare at the stars, count the planets, the universe smiles at me, i see the moon being master & servant, i see six sea serpents & six blackhawks looking like shadows

& then he crashed out the sky, with nothing, no name, no breath, no voice, naked, hoping to come home to a better world, to a better me & when he arrived

he was so beautiful.

# ODE TO THE COLONY

here in the colony
watch how history unfolds
     how ruthless america has been
     how they conduct themselves in public
        see how they defend themselves
        for their counter intelligence actions
for freedom fighters who have been
shot in the back, betrayed by greed
     jailed for dozens of years &
     for defending the liberation of this island
        those who gave up their humanity for
        a badge for career & a promotion
here in the colony, we see your names
attached to our tumultuous history
     destroying patria by abandoning towns
     demolishing buildings & closing schools
        they sabotage our lives in the dark
        they name the streets after heroes
who fought for independence, erect statues in their likeness,
desecrate their legacy & remind us that machine guns
     aren't holding flowers, these atrocities
     of corruption & evil are found on the state capital
        here in the colony, the procedures are deemed
        they destroy in the name of progress
but progress isn't in the embrace of
 capitalism or laying with corruption
     the only love is love of profit
     watch as the bulldozers destroy
        the memory of another neighborhood
        to build another monstrosity
& instead of helping un hermano de la patria
they sell the remaining assistance to the highest bidder
     they lack compassion for the liberation
     push bayonets in our stomachs
        in the name of our progress
        welcome to the colony.

# THE AMAZING DAY

this is the day
we rise up
in the morning
full of wonder
staring the sun
grateful for dreams
of the night before
still intact like a crystallized spiderweb
we heard no gunshots last night
we heard no screams
& the mirror showed us
an older version of ourselves

this is the day
nothing breaks
nothing will break on us
not our hearts, our lives
our family, our bodies
our homes, our children
we'll grow from every scratch,
fall, slip with no genetically
modified assistance
no corporate sponsorship
no breaks, crack, gash, split, rift,
rupture, fracture, tear but only cures
revivals, renovations, reinventions
renewals & regenerations

we will be full of miracles
no heart attacks, no diseases
no alzheimers, no hiv, no small pox
no std's, no diabetes, no influenza
no chemical labs of destruction
no pharmaceutical business
profiting off our sickness
there will be no sick

this is the day
no one will get shot or killed
we'll be bulletproof, foolproof
& celebrated like a shining saturday night

we'll grow flowers from our palms
find pens that never run out
hear our enemies say they love us
all the trains & buses will be on time
no worry about our bills
there will be no bills
& our bank accounts
will be sexy

this is the day
that being optimistic
is not look at strange
not looked at as delusion
but necessary as breath
like a paid lunch break
poetry is fed with pan y café
where art is cultivated
by everyone even by people
who don't enjoy it but
understand the need for it

this is the day
we create new harmonies
for the new songs for
our new skin with new eyes
so that we can be seen new too
we'll become independent
of any government or doctrine
we'll destroy all the jails
build more schools
build more gardens
we'll plant so many flowers
we'll tear down all the empty

condos & skyscrapers
build parks in their place
build homes to love in
reclaim these lands
in the name of people
we'll free the people
rehabilitate the concept
of freedom & rescue
those who have trouble
understanding themselves
it'll be fantastic

this is the day
there'll be no policing
of our bodies
we can be anyone
pick & choose
the dreams of our own making
with no judgment, no stigma
we can love & be with anyone
no supremacy of any kind
no hatred, no racism
no bigotry, no sexism
no homophobia, no transphobia
no banks, no capitalism
no republicans or democrats
no politicians or presidents
no dictators or monarchs
& no gods

this is the day
we forgive our loved ones
for not being loved ones
but we'll still accept them
& accept ourselves
because we are
flawed immensely
but still pure visions of joy

this is the day
no one goes hungry here
there'll will be no gluttony
no starvation or commercials
about feeding a child
no throwing food out
if not purchased
water is free      air is free
food is free      love is free

this is the day
we become more human
more humble with ourselves
use our imagination for
beautiful moments
we'll discover how
our emotions work
how we'll hold ourselves
more accountable &
give ourselves time
to understand how
love changes us
every time &
we'll be grateful
that we made it this far

this is the day
we'll explore every
inch of the world
travel the universe
see how everything is connected
& how we were wrong
about everything
how we are a microcosm
of a microcosm of a microcosm
& we'll restructure our ego's
because it made us think
we were the center of the universe

but we were light years
from the center
that we'll feel foolish
but yet with no shame
because being a part
of the universe is nothing
to be ashamed about

this is the night
we lay down
in the evening
full of wonder
staring the moon
grateful for for the day
spiderweb still intact
& crystallized &
we heard no gunshots
we heard no screams
& the mirror showed us
an older version of ourselves
& we found it amazing
so, so amazing.

# IN THE SHADOW OF
# THE AMERICA

we all arrive with an alphabet alter ego
      bald eagles, bursting bombs, black bags
blackbox, & the boogeyman is alive
      the chatterbox calligraphy is a catastrophe
cameras capture the cheap smiles of the commander
      the deep six database is the devils delicacy
designed by drunks & doctors
      even the echo is an exclusive elixirs for enigmas
electroshock elegance during the emergency exits
      fables face-off in freak factory, foolish fast breaks are
the favorites of the felonious fever pitch fetishes
      god is a ghetto genius ghost-dance full of gadgets
habitual hail mary's hallelujahs our haikus as hallucinations
      iambic iconoclasts immaculate in utero illusions
jabberwocky jargon jigsaws the jockstrap of the jingo
      kamikaze kaleidoscope kicking kingpins
label the labyrinth, lament your liberation
      lure the lullaby, dilute the language
mock the majority madcap magna carta machine
      narcissus is naked & narrow minded
observes the off peak officers opiates over the table obituary
      pacemaker politicians are a pale palette to frame
the parliament's paper patriarchy postures like plastic
      question the quantum-leap quotas
question the quartz quicksilver quads
      the robots of reaganomics revolt against reality
resurrected reactionary rhetoric reclaim the reservations
      the sadomasochists secret service their safety sex
safety pin salvation, salivate the seduction
      semiautomatic shotgun siamese sideshow sacrifices
take-no-prisoners telenovela, the tanks & topless
      technophile tourniquet the trojan horse
uncivil, unusual, undecided & unbelievable to be united
      the vile vermin's venom sealed in vellum

vexed in their vehicles carry volcano sized vengeances
      who worries about witches & werewolves?
xenophobic xylographs & xanax xylophonist
      yesterday yanked the youth
yesterday the youth saw the years
      zenith the ground zero for zombies & zealots
zenith the ground zero for zigzags & zodiacs

      welcome to america
      where we stand in the shadow of goliath
      where the orchestras play out of key
      where they protest & parade against liberation
      where your passport gets national revoked
      where we wear social security like jackpot numbers
      where everyone is wallflower paper no one likes
      where everything is a song & dance with bad music
      where you'll need a monkey suit to show off
      where you'll feel right at home dancing for spectators.

# THE ADVENTURES OF FELA

I. *The New Routine*

tonight
i sleep on a
bed that is not mine, in
a room i did not decorate,
people

who work
here, i do not
know their names, they call me
by my surname, patient number
my chart

this has
been a long road
everything hurts, feels broken but
i'm patient, i know it seems like
it won't

ever
stop, but it won't
last forever, i think
of how my body has failed me
betrayed

me for
sweets, gave me high
blood pressure, developed
new routine of pills, insulin
but this

will not
be my song, this
will pass, diabetes
is another chapter in my
life like

deadbeats,
migration, like
single parenthood, like
wild child teenagers, this too will
soon pass

II.*Remembering Papa y Mama*

i found a picture
of the two of you
sitting on a couch
plastic & glorious

papa, your six foot four frame
& caramel complexion
so familiar to my own
even though my children
do not have your melanin

mama, so petite & strong
what a shining star
you are, i'm glad you
didn't see me during
decades of dyed hair
& short buzzcuts

i remember how your angry smirk
looked like a pack of hyenas

you two stayed together
in guánica in little shack called home
how did you do that?
i couldn't even keep
the house in levittown

papa, primero trabajaste
coltando caña then
i remember you

playing the guitarra in the campo
did you know your guitar
is in a museum in town square

both of you originally
from sabana grande[56]
settled in guánica
never left there
never visited san juan
or new york

papa, my son plays guitar
& one of my grandsons plays cello
let's hope your love
for playing streamlines
into all the generations
i am keeping my fingers crossed
my grandsons are beautiful boys
talented, athletic, brilliant boys
i wish i saw them more

papa y mama,
i miss your wisdom so much
i wanted to tell you
how much i miss you
your daughter, my mother is good
not the easiest person to deal with
but she helps when she wants
& is still here, i love her to death

i'm happy i found this photo
& had this conversation
with you two

te amo
tu trigeñita

fela.

III. *The Mountain*

i brace myself
daily, since my
deterioration
my son started
to hold me like
a baby in his arms
my young sixty four
year old frame
newly released
from the hospital
my body now bearing
amputation scars
but my heart & mind
is what he takes care
of the most when
he watches me
take slow steps
from couch to bed
i brace myself
for the outbursts
of agony & pain
that i hear in my voice
sounds like regret
sounds like should've
done something earlier

i brace myself
for the mountains
of medications
i have pick up from
the pharmacy
the same one
where they knew
lefty by first name
at first glance
they see him in my son

& they ask us how he's doing
& i'm the one who
has to tell them he passed
& that i'm picking
something up for me
i'm never prepared
properly for the look
in their eyes
& the apology
in their irises

i brace myself
when i cry
i cry in front of him
we are the most similar
the most emotional
i feel comfortable
enough to forget
he is my son
& see him as
someone who is
willing to help
willing to listen
willing to watch
old television with me

there are times
i am not strong enough
i pour sugar in my oatmeal
where he screams
at me as if i am his child
when he sees my addiction
to sugar in my sweet tooth
knowing damn well
that it put me
in this position
but i haven't sworn
it off forever, yet

he tells me
i am still
a woman
even though
i'm missing
my right toes
& half my left
leg is gone
he tells me
i still have
a life ahead

he hears me crying
at night from
the neuropathy
& climbs into
bed with me
like he did as
a little boy
i rub his head
i hate to be touched
so he kisses me
on the forehead

i am
bracing myself
for when
it's time for
the transition
i'll be grateful
that he'll be there
when i need
me the most

i'll be grateful
that i've lived
a life this long
& beautiful.

IV. *La Bata*

my mom's old house bata
has more history
than her entire closet
each spot & each stain
is a memory is a story
but its not really a bata
it's a really long shirt
but for the sake of
not upsetting her
we'll call it a bata
on the front
it has the words
of her hometown
            guánica
written on the back
of the shirt (or la bata)
& there's a drawing of
a random corner of the town

i ask her
            where's is this?
she looks at me & says
            how the hell do i know?
well, you lived there
            dejame vez, ehhhh it looks fake

that night
we rummage
through her closet
& counted 77 shirts
in her possession
that do not fit

i tell her she should
through them out
she yells no!

she says i should give
some of my clothes away
i tell her give away your 80's wardrobe
       she yells you're crazy! as if i didn't work
       for all these clothes
you mean the ones
that will eventually be batas
       callate la boca, puñeta!, carajo!
       they're mine y ja

my mom's old house bata
has so many stories
so many melodies
everything from elvis presley[57]
to ismael rivera[58]
she tells me these little anecdotes
that i think she's making up on the spot
       you know i saved your father in this bata!
       save him from what?
       i don't remember that's not the point

if she could stay
in her bata all day
& it be socially acceptable
she would & my mom is not
an old fashioned lady
she's very post modern
but the older she's gotten
she's developed old fashioned
lady tendencies
& i'm ok with that

my mom's old house
bata is older than me
& i'm happy
she hasn't thrown
either one of us away.

## V. *The First Words*

i went to visit my mother yesterday
& found her on the floor
the first words out her mouth
were thank god as if time is
a demon torturing her

i asked her, how long she was on the floor
& she was too embarrassed to say
i placed my hand on her head
said don't worry & helped her up

it's a visceral moment when i see my mother
who's always been a symbol of independence
is handicapped by the repercussions
of her decisions, its been two
years since her amputations
before that she was bed ridden
fighting neuropathic pain daily
trying her best not to scream

now she's a walking medicine cabinet
     pills for heart condition
     pills for arthritic shoulder pain
     pills for blood pressure
     pills for diabetes & sugar levels
she tells me they keep things even keel

growing up my mother
was the sharpest switchblade i knew
she can cut a moment with
a swift slice to my face
she could destroy me
from 100 feet with a stare
i remember her whippings
like a constant looped apocalypse
& some people would say

that's not cool she beat you
but in hindsight, i don't see it that way
i forgave my mother a long time ago
she never gave up on me & i've seen
parents give up on their children

i lift her off the ground
being what some would
call a good son but
to me it's about love
you can be a good son
& not love your mother
& vice versa

when she lost her ability to walk
i wanted to give her a new pair of legs
strong, firm, so she could run a race
like she used too, walk & wander
& rediscover herself again

after her retirement
the last few years
have aged her so fast
my once modern little mom
who talks about ~~ikea~~ & ~~walmart~~
all of a sudden was now
a little old lady in a wheelchair
who talks about ~~ikea~~ & ~~walmart~~

i went to see my mother yesterday
& found her on the floor
with a look in her eyes like
time was demon torturing her
the first words out her mouth were
thank god

the first words out of mine were
mami, it's alright, i'm here.

VI. *The Matriarch*

in the liberated shell of a man
my dead lover is not as intangible
as i would like to think
he is still a name my children carry

i deter those who find my family history
entertaining or interesting, it is neither
it is minuscule because the patriarch
was minuscule & i, the matriarch

carry a different name unceremoniously
i've been head of the family from day one
even though i thrived & forced this family
up by my boots, i am bogged down

by the memory of him, by this man who was
more burden than anchor, weighs us down
with the sound of his name but he is now silent
the patriarch is dead even though this house

never truly had a patriarch, he is now a memory
my childhood lover is dead, my children's father
is dead, my ex-husband is dead & i have remained
still like a pillar, strong & tall even for my five foot frame

i'll forever celebrate myself
like i always have
long live the matriarch.

# WEST SIDE MAYAGÜEZ BLUES

wake up in la plaza colon
the gallinas sound like
a reggaeton song

i can see the
storm creeping

i get into a taxi cab
to take me to el colegio
he's wearing a knicks hat

the car has no air conditioning
& a car in puerto rico
with no air conditioning
is another form of torture
i've nicknamed the car
the death trap

i roll down the windows
on both sides to create
a wind gust of hope

i'm now stuck in traffic
it's drizzling a bit
i'm dying slowly
of heat exhaustion

i jump out
& realize walking
will be faster
i step inside
of a rex cream
indulge in
fresa & piña
mango & maiz
they are all delicious

i'm searching for
the mustache of
eugenio maria[59]

i ride the sultana
bathe in aguas puras
run through parque del litoral
read poetry at la tertulia
dance on stage at teatro yagüez
drink at la naza on a tuesday
& watch people dancing
in the streets

i can feel the
storm creeping

edward shows me around
buys me more beers because
we are watching lebron james
dismantle the new york knicks
i drink a beer in less
than a minute
i tell him
  being a sports fan
  outside of the yankees
  is another form of torture
  like the taxi cab i was
  in earlier that day
they both makes me sweat
confused & exhausted
i bang my head on the bar
& scream at the tv

i can hear the
storm creeping

the lightning crackles
the humidity rises

the rain starts
comes down hard
i am waiting for it to end
edward tells me
       hey it could be worse
       at least you
       don't live here

the storm is here.

# AN ISLAND, DIVISIBLE

swollen fruit
dangle like
ripe memories
stretched across oceans
& forgotten flesh

here is a body
holding water yearning
to know freedom

boriken/borinquen
pre columbus    post columbus
pre america     post america
land of the     valiant lord

the 20th century
great migration
raised on mango
didn't understand
new colonial status
knew little english
remembers the gloucester[60]
knows the sounds
of machine guns
pre world war

duped & drafted
persuaded & persecuted
assumes only way out
is traveling to united states
lives through the great depression

from sabana grande to guánica
to bayamón to the bronx
dreams in spanish
speaks in english

both broken sentences
each family member
with a bag in hand
names in their back pockets
doesn't look like the movies
& didn't find anything except
basura y carros

six different shades
of boriqua sitting at a table
up north in a small apt. in the bronx

new nicknames, new friends on
american streets like alexander,
willis, bruckner, lincoln, morris,

the new barrio is
same as the old barrio
carry the same accent
pero no palm trees, no oceans
no isabela, no yauco
no ponce, no mayaguez
no aguadilla, no fajardo
no salinas, no caguas[61]

eventually everyone comes
to new york city at least once
feet worn, hearts bruised
salsa is a scarf everyone
wears on a saturday night
then hangs up for a sunday
of jesus christ hanging
in-between two vejigante masks

| big sister | surrogate mother |
| baby sitter | sibling caretaker |
| matriarchs | work at the cleaners |
| patriarchs | work at construction |

these city streets
once paved with cobblestone
now are ripped out & replaced
with black tar & concrete
  heroin & alcohol
   these are not the stories
   of a west side song & dance
   no time to sing, only work
   barely time to breathe

some move to new jersey
have more children
relocate to midwest
won't be seen in decades

some are vicious
find comfort at the bottom of a bottle
their name on the stool of a bar
greeted by a switchblade

some hold a temper like
needles next to demons
wild child until adulthood
makes odd decisions then
finds god but is still searching for self

some hold on to insecurities of
never being the favorite
never being the oldest
holds on to their wounds too tight

the buildings are so tall
the sun rarely peeks over
the same sun that rises over
the montañas in puerto rico
the same that rises out the atlantic
& sets beyond the pacific

the constant questions of the children
about themselves, about staying
about returning is all divisible

some return to puerto rico to return
some live in florida only to return
some never left new york city
some died too soon
some start with sienna
some start with sand
some die with worry
some die with hands

these bloodlines are
swollen fruit
dangle like
ripe memories
stretched across oceans
divided, separated
like forgotten flesh

119 years from
borinquen to
new york city

here are bodies
holding water
that knows freedom.

# TYPICAL CITY KIDS

our feet were tired & worn
from painting the streets
like a pack of wild wolves
we observed the chaos
that we tried to prevent
writing on these walls with bright white
& apocalyptic black
we are scarred & beautiful &
we write our brother's name
       in memorial

distance is never an issue
we see the sun rise in battery park
& walk up broadway & watch
the sunset at fort tryon
we tighten up when we hear the sirens
we stare at the cop car
its a game of truth or dare
who flinches first, who curses first
in these late hours of possibility
we could get our jaw broken
or life taken during a house party broken up
       by a coward hiding behind a badge

this granite & concrete that
we've been built from the ground up
has our fingerprints all over it
& with these hands we created purpose
& hope in the face of despair
told our stories on the block
at the party, on the microphone
& we created a new tradition
reinvented ourselves with names like
burke, vaz, dage, sege,
doves, smirk, bzar & reals
       a set of typical city kids

we lived in a city that left us to die
& were mad when we didn't

in these hoods
they thought it would kill us
but we multiplied by the hundreds
developed a hard rock spirit of survival
because we know concrete & cinderblock
whole generations ran to the suburbs
& traded this skyline for cookie cutter towns
& now they help their kids
buy their experience back into
this city they left for dead
they found out that, us, the undesirables
     & delinquents made
       this city so f*cking beautiful

the boroughs are being sold
to every corporation transforming
new york city into an outdoor mall
& that won't make it beautiful
but make the city more sterile than it is now
& we created beautiful things from
the murk, mud, crack & liquor
transformed it into rhythm, art & dance
& everyone wanted a piece of it
we resurrected ourselves, lost a lot of people
along the way & we're still here
     still wandering until we find meaning
     still hiding in the shadows to save ourselves
     because we've been killed in broad daylight

so we defend the bronx, defend manhattan
defend brooklyn, defend uptown
defend queens & defend staten island
which was completely forgotten
     until it became the slums of shao-lin[62]

we grew up too fast
stole our childhood back
didn't know how to be adults
& learned that this city won't
let us grow old gracefully

we rendezvous on corners & intersections
where their names have been changed
our body language will tell you everything
we keep our tongues sharp & our wits quick
& while invaders move in we sabotaged
the dreams they're trying to live
it's all dead inside like every
new condo being built

& we observe the chaos
that we tried to prevent
& we write our brother's names
        in memorial.

# OPEN LETTER TO NYC

dear nyc,
you've let these idiots ruin you so much, let me tell you, the east
village in the mid 80's was the first to get swept by the new
money & raising rents no one called it gentrification back then
but thats exactly what it was, as soon as real estate brokers
called it the east village, the rent tripled, it was the east village to
the them but to those who have been here for 30 years it's has
always been the lower east side, these areas we called home
used to be last choice the only people who rented there did so
because they got the cheapest apartments in the city but this is
where we were born & raised, some would say rents still pretty
low, some being landlords & real estate leeches, capitalists with
no sense of community or partnership, the definition of low
has changed, some would say $700 was low for the city but at
one point it was higher than it's ever been, so when someone
says $1200 is low for the city but it was higher than it's ever
been, it feels like a boulder rolling down a mountain, some
would say it's finally happened down there, it went through the
burnout & the junkies & now there's action, that's the language
of gentrification, the infection & how it spreads, those burn
outs were our fathers, our uncles, our heroes & thats how we
created hiphop, punk, nyc hardcore, it wasn't created with
pristine walls & sterile trains, it wasn't created with cops on
every corner but when landlords speak of these spaces that
nobody wanted them, that it was a mess outside, they never
speak of how president ford gave up on nyc allowed it to go
bankrupt, they never speak about heroin & crack was poured
into these neighborhoods of color: hell's kitchen, upper west
side, el barrio, fort greene, prospect park, bushwick, the south
bronx, long island city, harlem, williamsburg & the lower east
side, all beautiful neighborhoods full of people of color before
gentrification, they never speak about how horrible a mayor ed
koch was or that dinkins was the first mayor who didn't care
for petty crime then guilani & bloomberg became puppets for
the rich for five consecutive terms, tenants speak about an area
evolving, everyone's going to have a complaint, they try align

themselves with old nyc with statements like "we just got tired of walking out of our apts & seeing drug deals on at every street" but people forget to mention the war on drugs & how it flooded the city with drugs & alcohol & the nypd, who have the audacity to launch stop & frisk, but these are not the first of their kind, in 1984 it was called operation pressure point arresting 2,007 people in the first month, in 1994 it was called quality of life then broken windows policy of urban decay, but everyone will agree, they'll never be another time like it: fordham road, 181st st. junction blvd. flatbush ave., fulton ave., 34th st. old 42nd st., coney island, victory blvd, the grand concourse, broadway, & washington square park, damaged masterpieces that were covered with a new coat of paint & sold to the highest bidder, these streets, these neighborhoods, these boroughs that we found things under the bricks, wrote our names on everything, we're always undesired, we wanted to see if we wrote it, would we exist, then come back months later to see if we still exist, nyc has changed so much, when i first started hanging out, i was 14 running around the village i was the only bronx boy, with upper west side art students, brooklyn & queens girls, scrawny dominicans kids from the heights, we was timberland, uptown nikes, backwards baseball hats, extremely baggy clothes & always wore a backpack, always, we rode the d train to tremont, rode the a train from dyckman, rode the f train to jamaica, rode the b train to coney island, survived the j train in the winter, was always patient with the 1 train, took the old brown m train to wyckoff, the 7 train to willets points & the c train used to go to the bronx, these were adventures i always thought were necessary, i always had epiphanies at 3am, or on late wednesday nights after a hip hop show on the corner in front of a bodega, i never found it dangerous, even if it was, it made me grow up quickly, gave me common sense, made me stay on my toes, on astor place, i loved women, cried over women & saw people destroyed by drugs, in 1995 on broadway there was a store called the wiz, before that it was a flea market called uniques where all the late 80's freaks & weirdos would congregate, when the village was "the village," most places i've loved in nyc are gone, swallowed by the inflated prices of the rising real estate, even the old baseball stadiums are gone, no more shea stadium or the house that ruth built, nows its a bank's name & a old name on a new building, the bookstores are gone, two boots on bleecker st. is gone, tower records on 4th street, there used to be a gas station on broadway & houston ave., i would stand next to the phone booths waiting for everyone, the phone booth, an extinct idol, along with tokens, the xxx theaters on 42nd street & playland arcade, i saw everything from drug deals to wedding proposals, & model hunts, i even saw david bowie & iman once walking around soho, everyone should walk down broadway, it's one of the most amazing magical streets in the world, people will sell you everything from cd's & socks, cyphers on every corners, rackers, boosters, lo-heads & graffiti writers, we would go to the nuyorican for an open mic, most streets were filled with run down strips of restaurant depots & failed stores but everything was home grown, everyone we knew was from nyc, a few from long island & new jersey, rarely were people from california, the midwest or the south, around 1999 thats when people started spreading & moving away from the east village to the rest of nyc, nyu didn't own everything below 14th st. yet, mcdonald's is the only thing that still remains, you had antique boutique & dome boutique, i spent nights in central bookings, ran from cops, nyc had grit, grime, slime & crime, it taught me how to read people in a second, after 2001 nyc changed, the yankees stopped winning  the world series, the knicks didn't have ewing, oakley & starks anymore, michael jordan retired, hip hop was not centered in new york city unless you count jay-z, biggie & tupac were dead, that wasn't new to us but our innocence was gone by 1997, nyc, you've allowed these things to happen in the name of progression, sold us out for reality shows, let disney own times sq., starved for tourist money, allowed nyc to be turned into a mall, allowed new york city to turn into a police state that protected investments & property, but nyc is so much more than property, we made it beautiful, at it's most ugly, so stop pushing us out, stop pricing us out, nyc, wake the f*ck up.

dead ass.

# TOWNSHIPS

adjuntas. aguada. aguadilla. aguas buenas. aibonito. allentown. añasco. arecibo. arroyo. barceloneta. barranquitas. bayamón. bridgeport. the bronx. brooklyn. boston. buffalo. cabo rojo. caguas. camden. camuy. canóvanas. carolina. cataño. cayey. ceiba. chicago. ciales. cidra. cleveland. coamo. comerío. corozal. culebra. dorado. el barrio. fajardo. florida. guánica. guayama. guayanilla. guaynabo. gurabo. hatillo. hartford. hormigueros. humacao. isabela. jacksonville. jayuya. jersey city. juana díaz. juncos. kissimmee. lajas. lares. las marías. las piedras. loíza. luquillo. manatí. manhattan. maricao. maunabo. mayagüez. milwaukee. moca. morovis. naguabo. naranjito. newark. new britian. new haven. orocovis. orlando. patillas. paterson. peñuelas. philadelphia. ponce. quebradillas. reading. rincón. río grande. rochester. sabana grande. salinas. san germán. san juan. san lorenzo. san sebastián. santa isabel. springfield. tampa. toa alta. toa baja. trujillo alto. utuado. vega alta. vega baja. vieques. villalba. waterbury. worcester. yabucoa. yauco. yonkers.

# LAST NIGHT IN SANTURCE

last night i read in the same streets
my father ran through
i imagine him with rafaelito,
junito, keko & jorge acting like
fools with all the best intentions

i see them running down
fernandez juncos posted up on
the corner asking girls how was their day
i hear junito be loud & obnoxious
keko & jorge lower their head
yelling at him "mira dejala"

i see them waiting for the bus
that will never arrive
i see them arguing over
who'll smoke the last cigarette
i see them be wild & innocent
but get singled out
make the wrong decisions
develop the wrong vices
i see them fighting people
who looked at keko wrong
who's always been the nicest one

i hear rafaelito tell them
he's joining the army
i hear the guilty & the gavel
as papi goes to jail
i dont even know what street
they're on anymore
it looks like avenida ponce de leon
but could be willis ave.

the barrios de puerto rico
always have similarities

an army of banderas
the smell of cafe en la manaña
a cuchifritos on the corner
a bodega owned by don carlos
with salsa music playing in the background
sounds like cheo feliciano[63]

last night i read in the same streets
my father roamed through
i saw him in his youthful abrasiveness
thinking he knew everything in the world
that he had everything planned out

& i want to walk up to him
tell him "mira papi, ten cuidado"
& say it like he would know i was his son
say it like i could change his future
even if that meant me not existing

i wanted him to have a such a different life
than he lived, like a character in a garcia marquez
novel not a greek tragedy or a crime noir
pero something magical

i tell him
"papi, there's so much for you to do in this world
don't go out with your friends tonight
call that trigeñita you met, fela ask her
what books does she like pero, stay home
& tell your siblings you love them,
play tag, pero don't go out papi
make better decisions
you're going to have kids
that need your love
you still have time
to change everything papi
to live a life that's beautifully amazing
to live a life left of everything you knew

last night i saw my father
in these streets of santurce

        i gave him a head nod
said whats up
but he didn't see me

he was busy chasing
the ghosts of his future

he didn't see i had so much
love & hope for him

he didn't see me at all.

III.

# IN THE MOURNING OF OUR INDEPENDENCE

since the beginning
men in ships thought
they found a paradise to conquer

we in one shape or another
have always been here
before america
before the west indies
before puerto rico
we've been through countless treaties
referendums & plebiscites created for us

we were still swimming
celebrating the new charter
the former oppressive country
signed to free us

this is what colonialism
looks like in the 19th century

boardrooms in suits
monopolize our lives
sell our island like commodity
cut of our supply
make some dependable on them
so when we speak of independence
we are looked at as crazy or radical

& we've rioted more than once
to try to control our destiny
to manifest our fate but as cannons
can be metaphors it doesn't hurt as much
as being betrayed by our brothers
for rank or position

at the turn of the century
self serving politicians
military generals & businessmen
who fought for the south in the civil war
the american indian wars & wounded knee
were appointed to govern puerto rico

at the turn of the century
we've been plantation, military location
export platform for corporation tax breaks
all that could be harvest has been harvested
& these corrupt businesses
have tried to own it all

the atrocities of the jones act[64]
drafted 18,000 puertooriqueños into world war one
operation bootstrap[65] sterilized a third of
the women by experimenting iuds & birth control
without their consent or knowledge

we were force fed migration
with images of new hope
new land, new opportunities
made some dependable on oppressor
made them think they should be grateful
that we lived here now under the boot of hypocrisy
call it democracy, promote liberty, justice
& free speech for all who those in command

there was once a gag law
law 53 called *la ey de la mordaza*[66]
made it a crime to sing a patriotic tune
to speak & write of independence
to hold assembly in regards to our political status
to display our flag that we love so much
this allowed police to enter anyone's home
to search & seize all property, without a warrant
this happened to us, & no one knows the stories

we have uprisings
& massacres on our hands
ponce, jayuya, utuado,
rio piedras, naranjito, peñuelas
arecibo & mayagüez[67]
& no amount of salt water
can clean the blood from them

our body is salon boricua[68]
new york city is salon boricua
chicago is salon boricua
philadelphia is salon boricua
orlando & miami is salon boricua
       they will continue to come for us
       send forty me after us. shoot us
       drag us out into the street
       then arrest us & say we shot first

how many have died for freedom?
do we know what being free is?
have we been in the embrace of the oppressor
so long that we think this is how freedom feels?
       we've been fed decades of systematic apathy
       thorough corrupt politicians & elections
       we'll be systematically tortured, declared insane
       after spending 25 years in jail

& if you're pro statehood then
you're searching for something else
because that will not solve anything only
fully assimilate us into the american fabric

this is what genocide looks like
in the 20th century

our parents never saw a free puerto rico
our children may never see a free puerto rico
our grandchildren may never see a free puerto rico

& some of us don't know how to swim
     & it should be a mandatory survival skill
     because there are sharks on land, in sea,
     in corporations, in everything
     & some people think i am a sinking ship
     & some will jump ship
     & other will sink with me
     & some will light a candle then swim to safety
     but we all need to know how to swim
     we don't need an imperial lifeguards
     or american surfboards

we've been a colony of the united states
for 119 years & some of us are fighting to be free
this island has been run into
a 70 billion dollars in debt

we don't control our export/import
the pentagon owns 15 percent of the land
& operates five atomic missile bases

english has been declared
the official language three different times
even though spanish is also a colonized language

the whole world recognizes us
a colony except for the colonizer
don't plan the future in the embrace of an abuser
this country does not care for us
vieques was bombed for over 50 years
no president from mckinley to trump
has ever given a shit about puerto ricans
no commission created by racist white politicians
that don't even know our political status
should ever speak on the future of puerto rico

this is what imperialism looks like
in the 21st century

albizu campos, betances, lolita lebron
rodriguez de tio, gonzalo marin,
matos paoli, & filiberto[69]
are rolling in their graves
oscar lopez rivera[70]
was in jail for 35 years
for fighting for liberation
viva puerto rico libre!
is not a slogan for a shirt
but for our hearts

so when you defend the oppressor
say that all happened in the past
things are different now
puerto rico is a commonwealth
people voted on it
       remember
       how we've been cut of our supply
       made some dependable on the oppressor
       so when we speak of independence
       we're looked at as crazy or radical

but we're not, we love the island
& we know that it's future won't flourish properly
under the control of an government
that mainly sees the island as a military location
& corporate tax break haven

those who have died
can't tell their story
but we are not dead
we are here right now
       living puerto rico
       being puerto rico
       loving puerto rico
pa'que lo sepas

this is puerto rico right this minute.

palante!
siempre!
palante!

# AFTERWORD

In March 2015, Shaggy Flores & i were invited to speak at the University of Puerto Rico-Mayaguez by Prof. Jose Irizarry for a symposium on our mutual friend Prof. Juan Flores who had recently passed, this book would've never come to fruition if it wasn't for that trip & the several trips after in the next couple of years. When i would arrive to the island, i would find myself in bars that heroes of mine would frequent, perform in high schools where friends had attended & remembered memories that were over 20 years old. i dedicate this book to everyone who's taken the time to love Puerto Rico with all its flaws on every level. i've traveled to more parts of the island in the last few years than i ever have before. Do i feel more Puerto Rican because of the visits? No, but i feel more like a Puerto Rican Poet which balanced being a Nuyorican Poet. i embraced Nuyorican, both culturally & artistically because of the influences of Pietri, Esteves, Piñero, Perdomo, Medina, & Melendez. i wasn't trying to reinvent my identity but after visiting the island as a teenager & being ridiculed for being from New York, i still had to find what being Puerto Rican was to me was, these trips did that. i am a part of the Puerto Rican Diaspora, every puertorriqueño is a part of The Puerto Rican Diaspora. i wrote some poems specifically for Puerto Rican residents to know that i see them, we see them & that they're not alone during this tumultuous time on the island. Thank you to those who stayed & thank you to those who left. Both decisions are difficult ones & were done for reasons only you need to understand. Thank you to everyone who took me to discover amazing places all over the island, east side to the west side. To all the bars, bookstores, restaurants, mountains, beaches & placitas, thank you. To all the professors, philosophers, teachers, painters, musicians, dancers, & poets, thank you. Thank you all for the inspiration, thank you all.

Bonafide Rojas
Bronx, NY
2017

# NOTES

1. Castillo San Felipe del Morro also known as Fuerte San Felipe del Morro or Castillo del Morro, is a 16th-century citadel located in San Juan, Puerto Rico. One of my favorite places to go, it's so old, it really does its best not to transport you to a time when Spain was the colonial ruler of Puerto Rico.

2. Vieques [Bje-'kes] is an island–municipality of Puerto Rico in the northeastern Caribbean. It lies about 8 miles (13 km) east of the Puerto Rican mainland. The island's name means "small island" in Taino. Vieques became the focal point of a series of protests against the United States' Navy due to its use of the island as bombing range & testing ground, which led to increased cancer levels in the inhabitants of the small island.

3. Levittown [Lev-it-town] is one of the of seven suburban developments created by William Levitt & his company Levitt & Sons. Located in Bayamón. i lived there before i started school in New York. We were the only family in that moved from my neighborhood.

4. Bayamón [Ba-yah'mon] is a municipality located on the northern coastal valley, spreading over 11 barrios. One of the few where i've lived in my life. It reminds me a bit of The Bronx in the way it's secluded, overpopulated & people think it's far from everything.

5. Bomba y Plena is Puerto Rican Folklore music that features call & response singing set to ostinato-based rhythms played on two or three squat drums called *barriles*. Bomba, is generally agreed that it was derived from West Africa through the slave trade in Puerto Rico. Plena is a genre of music that focuses on the narrative song that details the everyday life of people & the communities.

6. Jibaro [Hee'bar-oh] has been used to refer to the people of the countryside that farm the land in traditional ways. The jíbaro image serves as a representation of the roots of the modern day Puerto Rican & symbolizes the strength of traditional values as living simple & properly caring for homeland & family.

7. Cayey [Ka'yei] is a mountain municipality in central Puerto Rico located on the Centra Mountain range, it spreads over 21 barrios. It is notable for *Las Tetas de Cayey* & *El Monumento al Jíbaro Puertorriqueño*.

8. Guánica [Gwa'nika] is a municipality located in southern Puerto Rico, facing the Caribbean Sea. It is the historic landing point for The United States during the Spanish–American War. The invasion on July 25, 1898 led to Puerto Rico being obtained by the United States & has been a colony ever since. My maternal family is from Guánica & i spent many summers there as a child i could write a lot about Guánica from the Nazario's point of view but i am still exploring those stories.

9. Loiza [Lo'isa] is a municipality on the northeastern coast of Puerto Rico & spreads over 5 barrios. It's said to be the traditional birthplace of Plena along with Ponce. It also holds the yearly parade & celebration called *Máscaras de Vejigante*. Máscaras de Vejigante are a type of mask made in Loíza where people parade around wearing them, you can research more about why the masks are what they are, but i'll tell you they are beautiful but could scare children because it still looks demonic.

10. Santurce [San'tur-ze] is not a municipality, it is the barrio of my father's birth & most of his family, i don't know much about my grandfather died at 21 & my grandmother wasn't the type to share stories over coffee, bochinche yes, but stories no.

11. Nuyorican is a portmanteau of the terms "New York" & "Puerto Rican" & refers to the members or culture of the Puerto Rican diaspora located in or around New York City. The first time i heard the term Nuyorican was when my sister took me to The Nuyorican Poets Café in 1993. The first Nuyorican poet i read was Willie Perdomo & he was also the first Nuyorican poet i met. Read the afterword for more on Nuyorican.

12. Pedro Albizu Campos was the leading figure in the Puerto Rican independence movement. He was an attorney, the president & spokesperson of the Puerto Rican Nationalist Party from 1930 until his death in 1965. He was imprisoned 26 years for attempting to liberate Puerto Rico from United States imperialism. He's one of the island's greatest patriots & Lolita Lebrón called him Puerto Rico's most visionary leader.

13. Pedro Pietri, Jesus Papoleto Melendez, Miguel Piñero, Tato Lavieria, Sandra Maria Esteves, Louis Reyes Rivera, Jorge Brandon, Miguel Algarín, & Bimbo Rivas. These are just a few people who have influenced me from The Nuyorican School of Poetry. Some are well known, others are not, all are necessary. Without this group, Puerto Rican poetry in the diaspora would be drastically different.

14. Ramón Emeterio Betances was a Puerto Rican nationalist. He was the primary instigator of *El Grito de Lares* revolution & is considered to be one of the fathers of the Puerto Rican independence movement. Betances is also considered *"El Padre de la Patria."* Betances has so many connections to the Caribbean/Antillean identity of the late 1800's, that more of his work needs be translated.

15. Cabo Rojo ['Ka-bo 'Ro-ho] is a municipality situated on the southwest coast of Puerto Rico spread over 9 barrios. Its name derives from the reddish color of its salt-flats & the reddish tint that characterizes the seaside cliffs along its southern coast. It's one of my favorite pueblos in Puerto Rico, because of Playa Sucia & El Faro De Los Morrillos.

16. El Faro De Los Morrillos of Cabo Rojo is located in the southwestern tip of island. It was constructed in 1882 to guide passing ships through the Caribbean Sea through the treacherous Mona Passage into the Atlantic Ocean. The lighthouse is located over a white lime cliff surrounded by salt water lagoons & marshes. During my trips these last few years, i have gone to El Faro as much as i can. There is a serene beauty & peacefulness that you can't find in other places, its very seclusion & non-commercial development makes it worth the trip because the only things thats changed in the last 135 years are the seaside cliffs falling into the ocean.

17. The Mona Passage has two definitions: it's a strait that separates the islands of Hispaniola & Puerto Rico, connecting the Atlantic Ocean to the Caribbean Sea. The other is it's the name of my band. You might think this is self serving, but i chose to name the band The Mona Passage as a name after finding it in a dictionary & it felt right immediately. A rock & roll band named after a location in the Caribbean sea, i don't think it separates the two islands but connects them. Shout out to Mona island.

18. Río Piedras is not municipality but a barrio. It was a former municipality which was consolidated with the capital municipality of San Juan in 1951. It was founded in 1714, & has been the home of the University of Puerto Rico's main campus since 1903.

19. El Local is a dive bar, art gallery & music venue in Santurce.

20. San Juan [Sán 'Wan], Where to begin about Puerto Rico's capital? It's the most populated municipality in Puerto Rico.

It was founded in 1521 by Spanish colonizers who called it *Ciudad de Puerto Rico,* or "Rich Port City." Puerto Rico's capital is the second oldest European-established capital city in the hemisphere. It's generates the most income than any other municipality & has the most notable tourist sites. I'm not going to trash the capital because it can do it itself. Enjoy San Juan as much as possible but see the rest of the island too. It's so beautiful & you'll be surprised with what you find.

21. La Respuesta is a concert venue, alternative art space, & art gallery in Santurce.

22. Barry Allen & Wally West are fictional superheroes who appear in publications by DC Comics. Barry Allen is the second character to hold the mantle of the Flash & Wally is the third. Their power consists of superhuman speed & various other abilities such as intangibility, which are also attributed to their ability to control the speed of molecular vibrations. In 1985's crossover *Crisis on Infinite Earths,* Barry died saving the Multiverse, removing him from DC publications for 23 years & Wally took up the mantle of the Flash from 1986 to 2009. They are both currently The Flash & the debate on who's faster is always ongoing.

23. José De Diego was a poet, statesman, journalist, poet, lawyer, & advocate for Puerto Rico's independence from Spain & the United States. He's known as one the fathers of the Puerto Rican independence movement. De Diego is also historically popular for the proposed vision of the establishment of a confederation of the Spanish-speaking islands in the Caribbean known as the Antillean Confederation. It's romantic now to think of that concept with Dominican Republic & Cuba but excluding Haiti, Jamaica, The Bahamas & Turks & Caicos Islands from the Antillean Confederation is limiting its possibility. The political situation of each island is their biggest separator.

24. The Influences: if you're like me & ever wondered about a person's influences or who they read or admire, well here's my condensed list. Some have their own note, but not all of them because then this section would've been a lot longer. All you have to do is type their names in a search engine & voilá! Every single one of them could change your perspective & your life:
Ramón Emeterio Betances, Pablo Neruda, Pedro Albizu Campos, Ché Guevara, Martin Luther King Jr., Frida Kahlo, Salvador Dali, Joan Miró, Miles Davis, Malcolm X, Federico Garcia Lorca, Julia De Burgos, Anaïs Nin, John Lennon, Jimi Hendrix, Simon Bolivar, Jose Marti, Eugenio Maria Hostos, Toussaint Louverture, Emiliano

Zapata, Frank Zappa, Amiri Baraka, Allen Ginsberg, Jaco Pastorius, John Coltrane, Kurt Cobain, Jean-Michel Basquiat & Gabriel García Márquez. (word).

24. Camaradas El Barrio is a restaurant, gallery space & music venue in El Barrio, NYC. One of my favorite spots anywhere. Try the sangria with caution & excitement. I'm grateful for a Puerto Rican restaurant that supports community & is still in El Barrio during the constant gentrification of New York City. i've had book release parties, rock & roll parties & Mona Passage shows, it's a home away from home. (try the sangria, seriously!)

25. El Yunque National Forest is a tropical rainforest in northeastern Puerto Rico. Trails run to La Mina waterfall & Mount Britton, then up to the high-altitude dwarf forest. El Yunque is biologically diverse forests hosting hundreds of animal & plant species, some of which are found only here. Okay, now that you read that obvious brochure, just know it's really worth a visit.

26. Borinquen/Borikén is the indigenous Taíno name of Puerto Rico, which means "Land of the Valiant Lord". The terms *boricua* & *borincano* also derive from *Borikén* & *Borinquen*. It is a reference to someone of Puerto Rican heritage.

27. Viejo San Juan is the oldest settlement within Puerto Rico: the historic colonial section of the city of San Juan. It is one of the 2 barrios, in addition to Santurce, that made up the municipality of San Juan after 1864 & prior to 1951, in which Río Piedras was annexed. Viejo San Juan is located on a small & narrow island which lies along the north coast, & it's connected to the mainland by three bridges. It is bordered by the Atlantic Ocean to the north & to the south by the Bay of San Juan. Its character is recognized by its 16th & 17th Spanish architecture (narrow streets, cobblestone roads & brightly-colored painted buildings). I would say more, but Viejo San Juan is the epicenter of Puerto Rican tourist sites: it is beautiful, it is quaint & my mother likes to visit El Morro.

28. Boricua is derived from *Borikén* & *Borinquen* respectively, & are used to identify someone of Puerto Rican heritage. Which makes me question, why use both ethnic labels? Are we Boricuas? Are we Puerto Ricans? Yes, both, but you know where i'm getting at...right?

29. La Boriqueña has two songs by the same name. One is the official anthem of Puerto Rico after its commonwealth status in 1952, which begins "*La Tierra de Boriquen, donde he nacido yo, es un*

*jardín florido, de mágico primor...*" The second is the poem written by Lola Rodríguez De Tió in support of the Puerto Rican revolution in 1868. After the invasion & occupation of Puerto Rico, the United States deemed the revolutionary lyrics too subversive for official adoption; so a non-confrontational set were written in 1903 by Manuel Fernández Juncos.

30. Howdy Doody is a freckle-faced boy marionette & starred in The *Howdy Doody* show that ran from 1947-1960.

31. Bad Brains was formed in Washington, D.C., in 1977, they are widely regarded as one of the pioneers of hardcore punk. Bad Brains is positive mental attitude, are F.V.K., they're The Big Takeover, they're Banned in D.C., & i'll say it once & for all they are "The Greatest American Hardcore Band."

32. Led Zeppelin was an English rock band formed in London in 1968. The band's heavy, guitar-driven sound, rooted in blues & psychedelia on their early albums, has earned them recognition as one of the fathers of heavy metal. By the time i was 21, i had every single Led Zep album. So should you.

33. At The Drive-In is a band from El Paso, TX & features two of my favorite musicians Cedric Bixler-Zavala & Omar Rodríguez-López. Pick up *In-Casino Out* (1998), *Vaya* (1999), & *Relationship Of Command* (2000) & *in•ter a•li•a* (2017)

34. The Mars Volta was a band from El Paso, TX & was created by Cedric Bixler-Zavala & Omar Rodríguez-López. The Mars Volta didn't care much for boundaries or limits, they sang in Spanish & English on the same song & had salsa bridges in rock songs that were over 10 minutes. You could find so many influences in their music & it'll still be their sound. One of my favorite bands of the last 40 years. Listen to *Deloused In The Comatorium (2003), Frances The Mute* (2005), *Amputechture* (2006), & *The Bedlam in Goliath* (2008).

35. Talib Kweli is a hip hop artist, & a social activist from Brooklyn, NY. Kweli is a lyricist after my own poetic heart. Nkuru Books Forever! Listen to *Mos Def & Talib Kweli Are Black Star* (1998), *Quality* (2002), *The Beautiful Struggle* (2004), *Eardrum* (2007)

36. Common is a hip hop artist, actor & activist from Chicago, IL. Common's done so much work i don't need to go into depth but *Resurrection* (1994), *One Day It'll All Make Sense* (1997) & *Be* (2005) are my favorite albums.

37. Mayagüez [Mah-yah'gwes] is a municipality of Puerto Rico. It spreads over 21 barrios. One of the barrios is Mona Island

& Monito Island. This is the largest ward by land area, & at the same time the only one without any permanent population. It's located in the center of the western coast of Puerto Rico. Founded in September 1760. It's the fifth-largest city & is considered one of the most important cities in the island. Home to University Of Puerto Rico-Mayagüez campus. Beware when Las Justas are happening, just saying.

38. *"Buen provecho"* is a popular term said before eating any meal. It is a loose translation of *Bon Appétit* but i feel *Buen provecho* has a blessing attached to it. So, if you're at a Puerto Rican restaurant prepare to say it & have it said to you.

39. The Fania All-Stars is a musical group formed in 1968 as a showcase for the musicians on Fania Records, the leading salsa record label of the time. The Fania All Stars had some of the best Latino Music performers in the world. At one point or another the line-up consisted of: Ray Barretto, Joe Bataan, Willie Colón, Larry Harlow, Monguito, Johnny Pacheco, Louie Ramírez, Ralph Robles, Mongo Santamaría, Bobby Valentín, Singers: Hector Lavoe, Adalberto Santiago, Pete "El Conde" Rodriguez, Ismael Miranda, La La, Ray Maldonado, Ralph Marzan, Orestes Vilato, Roberto Rodriguez, Jose Rodriguez, Barry Rogers, Tito Puente, Eddie Palmieri, Ricardo Ray & Jummy Sabater.

40. Shazam also known as Captain Marvel is a fictional superhero who appears in publications by DC Comics. He is the alter ego of Billy Batson, a boy who, by speaking the magic word "SHAZAM" can transform himself into a costumed adult with the powers of superhuman strength, speed, flight, & other abilities.

41. Solomon, Hercules Atlas, Zeus, Achilles, & Mercury are the 6 Greek Immortal Elders that grant Billy Batson/Shazam his superhuman powers.

42. Roberto Clemente was a Puerto Rican professional baseball player. From Carolina, Puerto Rico, he was involved in humanitarian charity work in Latin American & Caribbean countries during the off-seasons. On December 31, 1972, he died in a plane crash while *en route* to deliver aid to earthquake victims in Nicaragua at the age of 38. He was the first Puerto Rican & Latin american inducted into the National Baseball Hall of Fame in 1973. MVP. All Star. Legend. Number 21

43. The Black Panther Party is a revolutionary black nationalist & socialist organization formed in 1966, in Oakland, CA. The Black Panther Party's core practice was to arm its citizens'

& to patrol & monitor the behavior of the police departments & prevent police brutality. There were chapters in all major cities New York, LA, & Chicago. They published a newspaper called *The Black Panther*, served as security escorts for Betty Shabazz & created The Ten-Point program & published it in the second issue of the *The Black Panther*. The first point: *"We want freedom. We want power to determine the destiny of our Black Community."* Find the rest of The Ten-Point program & read it.

44. The Young Lords Party was a Puerto Rican nationalist group formed in 1968 in Chicago, IL & in New York in 1969. They addressed issues concerning prisoners, women, the working poor, Vietnam war veterans & high school students. They summarized their political beliefs & goals in a 13-point program, published & distributed a newspaper called *Palante!* The Young Lords supported independence for Puerto Rico, all Latino nations & oppressed nations of the world & also neighborhood empowerment. This original symbol with a map of Puerto Rico & a brown fist holding up a rifle & the purple lettering reading, *Tengo Puerto Rico en mi Corazón, "I have Puerto Rico in my heart."* The Young Lords addressed local & national issues of police injustice, health care, tenants' rights, free day care, free breakfast for children, & a more accurate Latino education.

45. Loisaida : [Lo-ees'sai-dah] is a term derived from the Spanish pronunciation of "Lower East Side." Originally coined by poet Bimbo Rivas in his 1974 poem "Loisaida", it now refers to Avenue C in Alphabet City, whose population has largely Puerto Rican influence since the 1960s now is an encompassed a wider Caribbean & Latin American community.

46. Kendrick Lamar is a hip hop artist from Compton, CA. One of my current favorite hip hop artists, listen to: *Good Kid, M.A.A.D City* (2012), *To Pimp a Butterfly* (2015), & *Damn* (2017).

47. PJ Harvey is an English singer & musician from England. Instead of saying how much i enjoy her (because i love PJ Harvey) i'll list my favorite albums instead: *Dry* (1992), *Rid of Me* (1993), *To Bring You My Love* (1995) *Stories from the City, Stories from the Sea* (2000), *Uh Huh Her* (2004), *White Chalk* (2007), *Let England Shake* (2011).

48. Stevie Wonder is a genius & you should already have a large collection of his work. Start with these records: *Music of My Mind* (1972), *Talking Book* (1972), *Innervisions* (1973), *Fulfillgness' First Finale* (1974) & *Songs in the Key of Life* (1976)

49. Radiohead is a rock band from Oxford, England, another band you should already know & own a few records. My recommendations: *The Bends* (1995), *OK Computer* (1997), *Kid A* (2000), *Hail to the Thief* (2003), *In Rainbows* (2007), *A Moon Shaped Pool* (2016). i should point out that Radiohead is one of my favorite bands of the last 40 years, if not my favorite. *OK Computer* is always a top 3 choice on my endless compilations of music listing.

50. Willie Perdomo is an award winning Puerto Rican poet. His books: *Where a Nickel Costs a Dime, Postcards of El Barrio, Smoking Lovely* & *The Essential Hits of Shorty Bon Bon* have inspired me & generations of poets. Willie is the truth & will always be the truth.

51. Patricia Smith is an award winning American poet & performer. *Blood Dazzler. Shoulda been Jimi Savannah. Incendiary Art. Teahouse of the Almighty. Close to Death.* Get your life right: Patricia Smith is a legend.

52. Lucille Clifton was an award winning American poet, playwright & author. She was Poet Laureate of Maryland, & published over two dozen books, read *Blessing The Boats* & *The Collected Poems of Lucille Clifton* then find all her books, consume them then breathe.

53. Aracelis Girmay is an award winning American Poet. She has three collections of poetry: *The Black Maria, Kingdom Animalia,* & *Teeth* & you should own all of them. Get it together Aracelis is an amazing writer & you're doing yourself a disservice. Go now! Find those books!

54. Tony Medina is an award winning Puerto Rican poet & author. He's published over a dozen books of poetry & children books & co-edited three anthologies: *Bum Rush the Page, Role Call,* & *In Defense of Mumia.* The first book i read of his was *No Noose is Good Noose* & i am always grateful for it. Pick up *No Noose is Good Noose* if you can & *Committed to Breathing, My Old Man is always on the Lam* & *Broke Baroque*

55. Jason Reynolds is an award winning American novelist & poet. His books: *When I Was The Greatest, Our Way, The Boy In The Black Suit, All American Boys, As Brave As You, Ghost* & *Miles Morales (Spider-Man),* so now you know, go buy these books & give them to kids who don't like reading & they will love it. Thank me later.

56. Sabana Grande : [Sah'Bah-na 'Gran-de] is a municipality of Puerto Rico located in the southwestern region. It spreads over 7 barrios. So my mother told me both my grandparents are originally from Sabana Grande then moved south to

Guánica & after doing some research i found out one of the original families that settled there was "Nazario de Figueroa." My mother's surname is Nazario, so what does that mean? Nothing to you but to me it lets me to know where my family tree starts in Puerto Rico. I also think its funny the literal translation for Sabana Grande is big bed sheet. I don't know whats funnier the English or Spanish translation.

57. Elvis Presley was an American musician. You know, Elvis. Well it's one for the money…

58. Ismael Rivera is a Puerto Rican singer & composer also known as "El Maelo". He's released over a dozen records & embodied the mix of bomba y plena with the Cuban son vocal singing style. With his carried a booming, precisely rhythmic, yet equally spontaneous voice, Ismael Rivera was a master.

59. Eugenio Maria De Hostos was a Puerto Rican educator, philosopher, lawyer, & advocate of the island's independence. He worked in the Dominican Republic as an educator. He joined the Cuban Revolutionary Committee & believed in the creation of an "Antillean Confederation." Hostos returned to the United States in 1899 & actively participated in the Puerto Rican & Cuban independence movements; his hopes for Puerto Rico's independence after the Spanish-American War turned into disappointment when his proposals were rejected & Puerto Rico was converted into a United States colony. Hostos is one of the great patriots of Puerto Rico. i greatly admire his effort in promoting Puerto Rican independence throughout the world.

60. The Gloucester was the first ship to set anchor in the bay of Guánica during the invasion of Puerto Rico by the United States during the Spanish-American War.

61. Isabela, Yauco, Ponce, Aguadilla, Fajardo, Salinas, Caguas are municipalities in Puerto Rico. They definitely deserve their own note but you can research too, you know. Here, I'll give you two:

Isabela [IsaˈBela] is a municipality of Puerto Rico located in the north-western region of the island & spread over 13 barrios. The town is known as *"Jardín del Noroeste,"* "Garden of the Northwest," because of the many wild flowers in its landscape. Isabel is a hybrid town, being a coastline city that has beaches but also mountains, rivers, lake, caves, cliffs, coastal flats & tropical forests & mangroves.

Ponce [ˈPonse] is both a city & municipality of Puerto

Rico located in the southern coastal plain region of the island, facing the Caribbean Sea. The municipality has a total of 31 barrios including 19 outside the city's urban area & 12 in the urban area of the city. Ponce is Puerto Rico's most populated city outside of San Juan, often referred to as *"La Perla del Sur,"* the Pearl of the South. Okay, now look up the rest yourself.

62. Shao-Lin is the nickname for Staten Island created by hip hop group Wu Tang Clan.

63. Cheo Feliciano was a Puerto Rican composer and singer of salsa & bolero music. A vocalist with a rare baritone among salsa singers, his deep voice & quick wit as an improviser made him a favorite with audiences. He sang with the Eddie Palmieri Orchestra & was a staple of the famed Fania Records. Cheo recorded fifteen albums for Fania. So, my mother once told me she was at a bar in New York & that Cheo bought her a drink & flirted with her & i looked at her & asked her "What happened after?" she said "Nothing i went back to the dancefloor" & i looked at her stunned like, you could've been a Cheo record called "La Trigeñita!"

64. The Jones-Shafroth Act of Puerto Rico was an act by the United States Congress, signed by President Woodrow Wilson on March 2, 1917. Itgranted U.S. citizenship to anyone born in Puerto Rico on or after April 25, 1898. It also created the Senate of Puerto Rico, established a bill of rights, & authorized the election of a resident commissioner. The act extended almost all U.S. laws to have the same force & effect in Puerto Rico as in the United States. Two months after Congress passed the Jones-Shafroth Act, Congress enacted the Selective Service Act of 1917 which based conscription "upon liability to military service of all male citizens." The year before they passed the National Defense Act of 1916 establishing the composition of the U.S. military. So with the Jones-Shafroth Act & a combination of citizenship & the expansion of U.S. laws to including the aforementioned National Defense Act imposed a mandatory conscription into the U.S. military on Puerto Ricans, precisely at the moment that the United States entered World War I. As a result, more than 18,000 Puerto Ricans served in the U.S. armed forces during World War I. Coincidence? Within 20 years of the United States invading Puerto Rico, they made it mandatory for Puerto Ricans to be in the The United States Military, in defense of their colonizer.

65. Operation Bootstrap is the name given to a series of projects which tried to transform the economy of Puerto Rico into

an industrial & developed one. The United States with what is known as the Puerto Rico Industrial Development Company set forth a series of economic projects that tried to evolve Puerto Rico into an industrial high-income nation. Initially touted as an economic miracle by the 1960s, Operation Bootstrap was hampered by the growing unemployment rate. As living standards rose, manpower intensive industries faced competition from outside the United States. It faced harsh criticism from civil rights groups when the government was exposed for testing experimental birth control & surgical sterilization without the consent or knowledge on a third of Puerto Rican woman.

66. *La Ley de la Mordaza* was approved by the Puerto Rican legislature on May 21, 1948. It resembled the anti-communist Smith Law approved in the United States in 1940 & was signed & made into law on June 10th, 1948, by Gov. Jesús T. Piñero. It became known as Law 53: it stated that it would be a crime to print, publish, sell, exhibit, organize, help anyone organize any society, group, assemble people whose intentions were to paralyze or destroy the insular government. Anyone accused & found guilty of violating Law 53 could be sentenced to ten years of prison & fined US $10,000 dollars. Law 53 was repressive & was in violation of the First Amendment of the US Constitution which guarantees Freedom of Speech. Law 53 was a violation of the civil rights of the people of Puerto Rico. Being a colony of the United States, Law 53 was created to restrain the rights of the Puerto Rican Independence Party & the Puerto Rican Nationalist Party movements in the island.

67. The Puerto Rico Uprisings & Massacres: Ponce, Jayuya, Utuado, Rio Piedras, Naranjito, Peñuelas, Arecibo & Mayagüez

The Ponce Massacre was an event that took place on Palm Sunday, March 21, 1937, in Ponce, Puerto Rico, when a peaceful civilian march turned into a police shooting in which 19 civilians, two policemen were killed, & more than 200 others wounded. Most of the dead were reportedly shot in their backs. The march was organized by the Puerto Rican Nationalist Party to commemorate the abolition of slavery in Puerto Rico & to protest the imprisonment of Pedro Albizu Campos, on sedition charges.

The Jayuya Uprising was a Nationalist revolt that took place on October 30, 1950, in the town of Jayuya, Puerto Rico. The revolt, led by Blanca Canales, was one of the multiple revolts that occurred throughout that day on the island against the United

States government in Puerto Rico. The Nationalists considers the United States to be a colonial power.

The Utuado Uprising was apart of the revolt against the United States government in Puerto Rico which occurred on October 30, 1950 in various towns in Puerto Rico. The revolt culminated in the town of Utuado, where five Nationalists were executed without a trial in a police station, it is now known as the "Utuado Massacre."

The Río Piedras Massacre occurred on October 24, 1935, at the University of Puerto Rico-Río Piedras. Police officers confronted & opened fire on supporters of the Puerto Rican Nationalist Party. Four Nationalist Party members were killed that day.

The Naranjito Uprising was led by José Antonio Negrón & The Nationalist Party revolted & attacked the police. They regrouped to the nearby mountains & formed a guerrilla group. They continued to raid several locations until November 6. When the National Guard attacked the house where the group was staying. Negrón escaped to Corozal, where he was arrested days later.

The Peñuelas Uprising was the first of the Nationalist Party. In the pre-dawn hours of October 29, 1950, the police department of Peñuelas surrounded the house of Melitón Muñiz Santos' mother. Melitón Muñiz Santos was the president of the Peñuelas Nationalist Party in the barrio Macaná, & the police were about to raid the house that Muñiz Santos was using for the Nationalist Revolt.Without warning, the police fired on the Nationalists in the house. A firefight ensued, killing three Nationalists. The Nationalists were arrested & accused of ambushing against the police department.

The Arecibo Uprising was led by Tomás López de Victoria. He ordered Ismael Díaz Matos to attack the local police station. Díaz Matos killed four policemen before fleeing. Fellow Nationalist Hipólito Miranda Díaz was killed while he covered the escape of his comrades. Díaz Matos & his group were captured & arrested by the National Guard.

The Ponce Uprising broke out in October 29, 1950, when Police Corporal Aurelio Miranda approached a car carrying some Nationalists & with fellow officers attempted to arrest them. A gunfight ensued between the Nationalists & the police. The Nationalist were arrested & accused of the murder of Aurelio Miranda.

The Mayagüez Uprising was divided into several units assigned to attack different targets. The Nationalist Party of Mayagüez was one of the largest. One of the groups attacked the town's police station. This unit joined the others in Barrio La Quinta. After police arrived, the men escaped into the mountains & avoided further casualties by using guerrilla tactics.

68. Salon Boricua was a barbershop owned by Vidal Santiago Díaz on 351 Calle Colton & Esquina Barbosa in Barrio Obrero, Santurce, Puerto Rico. Salón Boricua was often frequented by José Grajales & Ramón Medina Ramírez, both leaders of the Nationalist Party of San Juan, & often served as a Nationalist meeting place. Santiago Díaz also befriended party leader & president Pedro Albizu Campos, who himself became a regular customer. On October 31, 1950, unknown to Santiago Díaz, fifteen police officers & twenty-five national guardsmen were sent that very afternoon to lay siege to his barbershop. As they surrounded Salón Boricua, these forty armed men believed that a large group of Nationalists were inside & sent a police officer to investigate. Santiago Díaz believed that he was going to be shot by this officer & armed himself with a pistol. The situation escalated quickly. Santiago Díaz shot first & the police fired back with machine guns, carbines, revolvers, and even grenades. The firefight lasted three hours. It finally ended when Santiago Díaz received five bullet wounds, one of them to the head. A staircase also collapsed on him. This gun battle between one barber & forty heavily armed policemen & National Guardsmen made Puerto Rican radio history. It was the first time an event of this magnitude was transmitted live via the radio airwaves & the entire island was left in shock. Santiago Díaz did not die that day.

69. I have notes on Pedro Albizu Campos, Ramón Emeterio Betances, & Lola Rodriguez De Tio, so i'll focus on these four Puerto Rican patriots.

Lolita Lebrón was a Puerto Rican nationalist, who migrated to New York City in 1941. She joined the Nationalist Party & gained influence with the party's leadership. She advocated for socialist & feminist ideas within the Nationalist Party. In 1952, after the Constitution of the Commonwealth of Puerto Rico was established, the Nationalist Party began a series of revolutionary uprisings. Pedro Albizu Campos ordered her to organize attacks in the United States, focusing on locations that were the most strategic. She attacked The House Of Representatives in Washington D.C. for the liberation of Puerto Rico & with Rafael

Cancel Miranda, Irvin Flores & Andres Figueroa Cordero in 1954. She yelled *"Viva Puerto Rico Libre!"* When she was arrested she said *"I did not come to kill anyone, I came to die for Puerto Rico."* She spent 25 years in jail & was freed from prison in 1979 after being granted clemency by President Jimmy Carter. After their release in 1979, the Nationalists returned to Puerto Rico, where independence movements received them with a celebration. During the following years she continued her involvement in pro-independence activities, including the Vieques protests.

Francisco Matos Paoli was an acclaimed Puerto Rican poet, critic, Secretary General of the Nationalist Party & essayist. After the Nationalist Uprisings in Puerto Rico, on November 2, 1950, the police arrived at Paoli's home in Río Piedras & searched for guns & explosives. The only thing they found was a Puerto Rican flag but, due to *Ley De La Mordaza* (Law 53), this enabled them to arrest & accuse Paoli of treason against the United States. The evidence used against him was the Puerto Rican flag in his home, & the four speeches he'd made in favor of independence. On the basis of this evidence, Paoli was sentenced to a twenty-year prison term, which was later reduced to ten years. In jail, he shared his cell with Pedro Albizu Campos. In prison, Paoli edited a newspaper which included poetry, news of political prisoners, patriotic songs & drawings. During imprisonment he suffered from hallucinations & mental breakdown. Paoli wrote *Canto a Puerto Rico* (*I Sing to Puerto Rico*). In 1951, he published a collection of poems in a book which he titled *Luz de los Héroes* (The Light of Heroes), which spoke about the Puerto Rican independence movement. Paoli's poetry covered other aspects of human existence such as religion, mystic & spiritual experiences, love, death, solitude, social justice, suffering, freedom, the landscape, & Puerto Ricans. He was released on probation on January 16, 1952. Paoli published a dozen collections of writings & in 1977 was nominated for the Nobel Prize in Literature.

Francisco Gonzalo Marín was a poet & journalist who fought alongside José Martí as a member of the Cuban Liberation Army. Marín received the tragic news that his brother perished in the *Battle of Manigua* in Cuba. This motivated Marín to travel to New York City & enlist in the Cuban Liberation Army. The recruitment for the Cuban Army was situated in the New York offices of the Cuban Revolutionary Party. Jose Martí was registering the volunteers. During his stay in the city, he collaborated in the *La*

*Gaceta del Pueblo* a separatist newspaper which published the narrative *"New York from Within."* Marín is credited to have allegedly designing the Puerto Rican flag. He used the Cuban flag as a model & inverted the colors in the flag's triangle & stripes.

Filiberto Ojeda Ríos was the commander-in-chief of *Los Macheteros,* who campaigned for, & supported, the independence of Puerto Rico from the United States. Filiberto moved his family from Puerto Rico to Cuba in 1961 & founded & led the *Movimiento Independentista Revolucionario Armado* aka MIRA in 1967. MIRA was eventually disbanded by police & Filiberto was arrested. He went to New York, where he cofounded the *Fuerzas Armadas de Liberación Nacional* (FALN) with former MIRA members. In 1976, Filiberto founded *Los Macheteros* named after the sugar cane harvesters who use machetes to cut the canes. Filiberto's belief was that the establishment of the Commonwealth had served to provide an illegitimate & false consent to the territorial status, resulting in the elimination of agricultural production, displacement of local businesses by corporations & the application of obligatory service that served to serve both large scale wars & smaller interventions throughout the world. Focusing on the independence movement, Filiberto suggested a Constituent Assembly would be held to solve the issues once independence was achieved. On September 23, 2005, on the anniversary of *El Grito de Lares,* members of the FBI surrounded Filiberto's home in Hormigueros, Puerto Rico. Most of what the the FBI are *claims* so take this all with a grain of salt. The FBI *claims* it was performing surveillance. The FBI *claims* their surveillance team was detected proceeded to serving an arrest warrant against Ojeda Ríos. The FBI *claims* that as the agents approached the home, shots were fired from inside & outside the house allegedly wounding an agent. The FBI *claims* it then returned fire fatally wounding Ojeda Ríos. An autopsy of Filiberto's body determined that he bled to death over the course of 30 minutes. The Puerto Rico Civil Rights Commission started an investigation of the incident shortly after Filiberto's death that lasted 7 years. The 227-page report issued on September 22, 2011, stated that Filiberto's was "an illegal killing" by the FBI. His house still has the bullet holes in the walls. He was 72 years old when he was murdered.

70. Oscar López Rivera is a Puerto Rican independence activist. One of the leaders of the *Fuerzas Armadas de Liberación Nacional* (FALN). He was in the drafted into the Vietnam War & was awarded The Bronze Star for his service. In 1977, López

Rivera was arrested & for fighting for the liberation of Puerto Rico. López Rivera cited international law that he was an anti-colonial combatant & could not be prosecuted by the United States. On August 11, 1981, López Rivera was convicted & sentenced to 55 years in federal prison. The imprisonment of López Rivera was opposed by groups nationally & internationally. López Rivera & 13 other FALN members were offered a conditional clemency in 1999, but López Rivera rejected it. On January 17, 2017 President Barack Obama commuted López Rivera's sentence & is scheduled for release from prison on May 17, 2017, after 35 years in prison. Oscar Lopez Rivera had been incarcerated longer than almost any political prisoner. On February 9, 2017, he was moved from a prison in the United States to Puerto Rico, where he completed his sentence under house arrest. Oscar is home. Oscar is Free. Que Viva Puerto Rico Libre!

# ACKNOWLEDGEMENTS

TO MY FAMILY! John Pablo Rojas, i love you. Felicita Nazario, i love you, (the pudding man!), Katina Rojas Joy, Nate Joy, Ignacio & Diego Joy, i love you. TO MY FRIENDS! Vincent Ramirez, Angel Zenon, Fifi Perez, Kumasi J. Barnett, Joseph Perez, Pete Sustarsic, Joe Vega, Dennis Kim, Willie Perdomo, Urayoán Noel, Tony Medina, Jason Reynolds, Gabriel Ramirez, Randall Horton, Anthony Morales, Mariahadessa Ekere Tallie, Cheryl Boyce Taylor, Mayra Santos Febres, Reginald Dwayne Betts, Quraysh Ali Lansasa, Patricia Smith, Adrienne Maree Brown, Mike Ladd, Rich Villar, Luivette Resto, Ninja Ruiz, UNIVERSES, Defend PR, Adrián Viajero Roman, Eli Jacobs-Fantauzzi, Mikey Cordero, Christian Martir, Stephanie Llanes, Mariposa, Melle Sol, Charlie Vazquez, Latanya DeVaughn, Sydney Valerio, Peggy Robles-Alvarado, Cliff Notez, HipStory, Mikal Lee, Nkosi Nkululeko, Roya Marsh, Venessa Marie Marco, Mahogany L. Browne, Jive Poetic, Patrick Rosal, Jay Lee, Shihan Van Clief, Jeff Chang, Betsy Casanas, Sham-e Ali Nayeem, Edward Contreras, Joey Robles, Fernando Rodriguez Ayala, Ramon Valle Jimenez, Francisco Mojica, Ana Portnoy Brimmer, Fernando Correa Gonzalez, Nan Van Vicente, Maritza Stanchich, Nicole Delgado, Amanda Hernandez, Rock Wilk, La Bruja, Reynold Martin, Desiree Bailey, Jay Salazar, Tongo Eisen Martin, Thomas Fucaloro, Nabila Lovelace, Aziza Barnes, My TCK (Top City Krew), Fernando Reals, Charlie Doves, Vaz Avedian, Angelo Baque, Antonio Kel, Sege, Eric, Bzar, Smirk Chris Maestro, Olivia, Jacob, Angel Skunk, Orlando Plaza, G-Bo The Pro, Crazy Legs, Velcro, Fefito, La Respuesta, Ben Ramos, David Galarza Santa, Kahlil Jacobs-Fantauzzi, Samra, Mission, Ying-Sun Ho, Sake 1, Wayne Collins, Vagabond, Giles Li, Danny Thien Le, Alynda Segarra, Cedric Bixler-Zavala, Omar Rodriguez Lopez, Miguel Zenon, Wonway, DJ Irfan Rainy, Capicu, Papo Swiggity, Jani Rose, Urban Jibaro, Sol Collective, The Poet's Passage, Samuel Medina, Libros AC, Camaradas EL Barrio &

David Bowie, Phife Dawg & Prince
rest in peace.

# ABOUT THE AUTHOR

Bonafide Rojas is the author of *When The City Sleeps, Renovatio* & *Pelo Bueno*. He's the bandleader for The Mona Passage. He has been published in these anthologies, journals & blogs: *Chorus: The Literary Mixtape, Manteca, Role Call, Lost Orphan Project, TheThePoetry Series, Bum Rush The Page, Learn Then Burn, Me No Habla Con Acento, The Centro Journal, The Hostos Review, The Acentos Review, Palabras* & appeared on *Def Poetry Jam* & *Spitting Ink*. He's been written up in The NY Times, NY Daily News, Culture Trip's 10 NYC based Latino Artists to know, The Centro & La Respuesta Media. He has performed at: Lincoln Center, The Brooklyn Museum, El Museo De Barrio, Bowery Ballroom, The Puerto Rican Traveling Theatre, Rotterdam Arts Center, Nuyorican Poets Cafe, Busboys & Poets & Festival De La Palabra. The Mona Passage second EP is due out in 2017. He currently lives in the Bronx.

for more info:

www.bonafiderojas.com
www.grandconcoursepress.com
www.themonapassage.bandcamp.com

CPSIA information can be obtained
at www.ICGtesting.com
Printed in the USA
LVHW111739120123
736947LV00004B/591